Professor **Laurence Alison** is the Director of Ground Truth (www.ground-truth.co.uk), a research and training consultancy for military and law enforcement leaders, offering cutting-edge advice and tuition on how to make tough decisions in crisis situations.

He is the author of more than 200 publications including 10 books on critical incidents, offender profiling and interrogation, and his work has influenced high-risk decision-making and interrogation around the world. In 2021 he was awarded an MBE in the Queen's New Year's Honours list for his services to these areas.

Neil Shortland, who has a PhD in military decision-making, has worked with the UK Ministry of Defence studying military training and operations in Afghanistan, and established a multi-million-dollar research centre at the University of Massachusetts, Lowell (USA) on security and counter-terrorism.

Together Neil and Laurence have studied how people in extreme situations take high-risk decisions. Their work has taken them all over the world. Their theories of decision-making – specifically, how to overcome overthinking and decision inertia – have been published in academic journals and their critically acclaimed book *Conflict: How Soldiers Make Impossible Decisions* was published by Oxford University Press in 2019.

Laurence: To my son, Heath – 6 foot 4 inches, with size 13 feet – an unusually good problem-solver and lateral thinker (though he has the humility to never brag about it). I wish I had your patience with others and your inner calm (especially under pressure). Parents – never say you can't learn from your kids.

To the doctors and nurses at Alder Hey Children's Hospital who saved Heath's life when he was a breath away from being taken from us at nine months.

Neil: To Josephine Yuen and the $1 beer that changed my life.

Decision Time

How to Make the Choices Your Life Depends On

Laurence Alison and Neil Shortland

Sourcebooks and the colophon are registered trademarks of Sourcebooks.

This publication is designed to provide accurate and authoritative information in regard to the subject matter covered. It is sold with the understanding that the publisher is not engaged in rendering legal, accounting, or other professional service. If legal advice or other expert assistance is required, the services of a competent professional person should be sought. —*From a Declaration of Principles Jointly Adopted by a Committee of the American Bar Association and a Committee of Publishers and Associations*

Published by Sourcebooks
P.O. Box 4410, Naperville, Illinois 60567-4410
(630) 961-3900
sourcebooks.com

Originally published in 2021 in Great Britain by Vermilion, an imprint of Ebury Publishing.

Cataloging-in-Publication Data is on file with the Library of Congress.

Printed and bound in the United States of America.
LSC 10 9 8 7 6 5 4 3 2 1

Contents

From War Zones to Wedding Planning

'Time was against me, and I had to make a choice. Should I go down this street and risk being shot or should I keep on going and risk being blown up by an improvised explosive device?'

'I simply don't know what to do for the best. I want to have a big wedding with all our friends, but I also just want to be married, and all this fuss is getting me down.'

T HIS FIRST OF these quotes came from a member of the United States Armed Forces: we were asking him about the hardest decision he faced during a deployment in Afghanistan. He told us he'd had to choose between taking an unfamiliar route through a very violent part of town or doubling back down the route he had just taken – a move that is advised against as insurgents sometimes plant bombs on routes they have seen soldiers on. The second quote comes from a friend who was deciding between having his wedding in the next 12 months so he and his wife could start their married life together, have kids and buy a house or delaying the wedding by 12 months so that more people could make the long and expensive trip to Australia, where they were now living.

On the face of it, these decisions seem worlds apart – and in many respects they are. The first was thrust on a soldier in the heat of Afghanistan, in the midst of a (then) 18-year-long war. The second was faced by a couple sitting in a comfy three-bedroom flat in metropolitan Sydney.

Yet look at these decisions from a psychological stand-point and you find several distinct similarities. Firstly, neither decision maker had faced a decision like this before. Our soldier called the choice before him 'unique' and 'not one I had trained for', while our friend had never had to juggle wedding planning, let alone a wedding that involved hundreds of people flying across the globe. Furthermore, in both decisions, all options presented the decision maker with a chance of a good outcome and, equally, a chance of a bad outcome. For our soldier, either decision could have resulted in significant physical harm or the safe return to base. For our friend, either decision could have a negative outcome – delay the wedding, but you might find people still cannot travel, or get married now but forever regret that so many friends and family members hadn't been there to see you tie the knot. Equally, either choice could lead to a positive outcome – what is a 12-month delay if it means you get to have your dream wedding? Or maybe you have the wedding now, and even with the smaller guest list you have the day of your dreams with your nearest and dearest. And finally, in both situations the only way to know the outcome was to make the decision.

We have spent our professional careers helping soldiers, police officers, medical professionals and others in high-stakes environments make tough decisions when lives are on the line. Laurence's work on operational debriefing has seen him working on cases as diverse as planning for the London and Beijing Olympics; the response to the 7/7 London bombings in 2005; the way Europe's biggest ever non-wartime fire (at Buncefield in the UK in 2005) was handled; the disaster victim identification team's response to the Boxing Day tsunami in Indonesia in 2004; and the poisoning of Russian dissident Alexander Litvinenko in London in 2006, as well as countless other major homicide and serial rape investigations. Neil's first job was working at the United Kingdom's top science laboratory (Porton Down) where he helped soldiers prepare for their deployments to Afghanistan. Since then, he has worked with soldiers, police officers and senior decision makers across the world as they face a range of challenges in their roles.

Interestingly, the feedback we've often had from military, security and other leaders we've worked with is that while our training has been directed at their professional decision-making, our courses have also helped them make better choices in their personal lives.

And that's what led us to write this book – because we've realised that what we know helps people make the big decisions in their personal lives, as well as the urgent, life-or-death decisions in tense, wartime or security situations. In the chapters that follow we're going to take you through the building blocks of good decision-making: and that means the next time you're faced with a major choice that will determine your future, you'll be confident about how to tackle it.

Because one thing we truly know is this: all of us will find ourselves, at various points in our lives, at an important crossroads, where we must make a significant and potentially life-changing decision. It might be whether to move house, if we should leave our job or partner, whether to move to a new country, how we might help our elderly parents or children, whether to report an incident at work or if it's right to euthanise a pet.

We are also aware, both as scientists and as observers of the world, that the tendency for indecision is often the most damaging outcome. We see inertia all around us, and we believe it's the most potentially harmful element of decision-making. From people failing to leave unhappy relationships, to dithering over whether to change careers, to avoiding making lifestyle changes that would make for better health, decisions are not simply about *what* is decided, but also *when* – and inertia serves us poorly. In many of our most crucial moments, it is an inability to overcome the fear of action that causes the most damage and stops us from being our happiest, healthiest, most successful selves.

This book will help you to deal with the difficult decisions you'll face in your lifetime, informed by our research in the field with people making critical, high-risk choices. It explores the psychological conflict human beings experience when faced with situations where all outcomes look horrendous. It draws on interviews with soldiers describing real-life situations, as well as observations from hundreds of events where we've trained police officers, ambulance and fire service personnel to respond to high-stakes situations including simulated terrorist attacks. We have also drawn on debriefs we have done with first responders who have had to deal with *real* terrorist attacks, as well as experimental research in the laboratory, neuroscientific evidence and work from our own experiments into how soldiers and police officers make decisions.

Our methods are varied, but the question at the centre of all this is the same: how do we overcome fear, procrastination and avoidance in the face of internal conflict, in order to commit to a decision? This book will explain the processes that so often conspire to make your choices seem overwhelmingly difficult. We will help you understand the feelings you're likely to have around decision-making: because much of the time it isn't just about you, it's about human instincts and deep evolutionary tendencies. Learn to recognise them, and you'll be a lot better at working out what to do next when you find yourself facing a dilemma. It's our aim to give you a set of keys to understanding not only your capabilities around decision-making, but also the hazards you're very likely to encounter along the way. Once you've grasped these, you'll have dramatically upgraded your ability to act effectively, and in the way that's right for you.

But, to be clear, this book isn't about what you might call everyday decisions. No, it's about the 1 per cent of decisions that have the potential to change your life forever. We want to help you navigate your way when you find yourself at an existential crossroads, and each chapter that follows will give you the opportunity to become fully conversant with a structure you can use to improve your decision-making skills, as well as ideas on how to put them into practice.

At the heart of our work, and this book, are the four points of our 'STAR' model that will guide you through even the most difficult of crossroads. If you can master the processes we outline, we guarantee you'll be in great shape to take on big, life-changing decisions.

1. Stories and scenarios: figuring out exactly what you are dealing with (see Chapter 4). Expert decision makers identify a plausible number of 'stories' that diagnose the events they see unfolding, and the possible directions those events could take. Poorer outcomes are often the result of less able decision makers pinning their diagnosis on either (a) a one-and-only plausible explanation or, at the other extreme, (b) a huge proliferation of too many models that then become unwieldy. Novices either do too little or too much; elite decision makers, by contrast, have enough, but not too many, ideas about what is going on.

2. Time mastery: knowing when to act and when to hold back (see Chapter 5). Elite decision makers ask themselves this crucial question: 'Do I need to decide this now?' If the answer is yes, they commit to a course of action. If it's no, they seek more information to further clarify what they are dealing with. Novice decision makers fail to make effective use of time; either they act too slowly or they act too quickly.

3. Adaptation and assumptions: how to clarify and test the situation, what to ask for and how to challenge

assumptions (see Chapter 6). The expert decision maker will adapt their perception of a situation as new information emerges. They are what we call 'fluid thinkers', and they are able to move on quickly and test hypotheses. Novices tend not to examine questions or consider alternatives.

4. Revision and resilience: knowing when to revise a plan is crucial. You need to know when to change and you need to know when to stick. And when you've made that choice, you need to stay strong in the face of difficulty (see Chapters 7 and 8). Elite decision makers revise their course of action based on new perceptions of the situation – even when that revision might not be popular with others around them. Moral courage matters. Strong performers take care of themselves: that ensures they're better prepared for the crossroads life will inevitably bring, and then better able to cope when they embark on their chosen pathway.

Making a difficult decision is daunting; it's not surprising that those facing one often hold their head in their hands and say, 'But I just want someone to tell me what to do!' The trouble is, that method never could and never does work. The STAR model isn't about anyone telling you what to do; it's about understanding a process that will enable you to use the power you have to be an adept decision maker. When you're faced with a difficult choice, you need to search inside yourself as well as use the tools we'll be giving you in the course of this book: because one of the things we've learned is that the *best* decision is only the best decision if it is right *for you*.

The STAR approach is all about giving you the ability to embrace uncertainty, the courage to face up to hard decisions, the tools to optimise your approach and the skills to commit at the right time to the course of action that's right for you. You'll learn a way of thinking that will give you confidence to approach a crossroads with a sense of adventure and opportunity rather than dread, and you'll be able to deal with even tough decisions successfully, without being dragged down by endless worry and anxiety, firstly about what you should do and secondly about whether you're going to get things right.

CHAPTER 1

Decision Time

THE BOMB, PLANTED deep within a road tunnel, smashes the weekday afternoon into a thousand pieces in a single second. Everything is silent as the world stands still and waits for the human beings caught up in the explosion to begin to take stock of their unthinkable new situation.

Then the smoke – a whisper at first, then thick and black – begins to curl out onto the road, followed by bloodied and dazed individuals who have escaped from their cars. The noise of moans and cries grows louder before being drowned out, a few minutes later, by sirens as the first emergency service vehicles arrive.

No one would want to have to take charge of a disaster of this sort, but someone has to. And let's imagine it's you. How do you think you'd respond if you were in command of the emergency response to this situation? Let's assume you're the senior fire officer: you've just arrived on the scene and are responsible for directing operations from a mobile control centre that's moving into place close to the mouth of the tunnel.

At first, it's all pretty textbook. A team of first responders is inside the tunnel. Within a few minutes, walking casualties start to emerge, followed by more seriously injured people carried out on stretchers. There's no fire, but the tunnel is partially collapsed, and there's an imminent risk that more of the concrete roof could cave in. Firefighters report two or three fatalities, and others are seriously injured.

But then comes a new piece of information: there's been a 999 call from someone claiming to be the bomber.

And what he has to say is chilling.

The bomb that went off wasn't the only one, he tells the operator. Inside the tunnel there's a second device, and it's set to explode in 15 minutes' time.

In the blink of an eye, you have become responsible for a decision that's unenviable in the extreme. Are you going to act on this new piece of information? And if so, what will you do?

This is one of the scenarios we often use when running our training courses on high-stakes decision-making. We know our scenarios are tough: we lay them on the table and we see the faces of people who have many years of experience, as they consider what they'd do.

Usually what we find is they ask a few rapid questions before deciding to pull their staff out of the tunnel to avoid further deaths:

- How far in the tunnel are my staff? (roughly half a mile)

- How long until I can get more support? (20 minutes for more staff)
- Do we know how credible the information is? (no, source unknown)
- How many casualties? (not entirely sure, upwards of 30)
- How many are ambulant? (again, unknown, roughly over half)

You might have asked similar questions. What we haven't revealed is that we haven't even arrived at the really difficult decision. So, here it is: four minutes after you've started to pull your teams out of the tunnel, bringing as many injured people as is possible with them, you receive a message from a fire officer inside the tunnel: 'I'm with an eight-year-old girl. She's trapped by a metal girder. I need pedal cutters – if you can send some in, I'll have her out of here in a couple of minutes.'

And then he continues: 'I can't leave her here on her own. She's the same age as my daughter. You have to get me those pedal cutters.'

Now this is a really difficult decision.

What we find in our courses is that people want to ask more questions, and sometimes repeat ones they have an answer to or have already been told there is no more information on. How long is the tunnel again? Do we know if the girl is conscious? How credible is the intelligence about the second bomb?

Sometimes, we spend several minutes discussing these questions, but, in real life, that's time you wouldn't have. Because while you're prevaricating, that second bomb could explode at any moment – killing both the eight-year-old girl and the firefighter, and anyone else in the vicinity.

It's easy to see why people want to stall, why they want to ask more questions, why they're resistant to taking a decision. Because this is one of those decisions where you're damned if you do and damned if you don't.

Let's press pause for a moment on our tunnel disaster and ask what makes a decision like this so incredibly difficult. When we tested it on fire officers during one training session, it led to stand-up arguments about what was the best course of action. There are no easy answers – here are the conundrums:

1. This scenario will to force you, under conditions of dire uncertainty, to choose between two options, both of which have the potential to be very, very bad.

2. It requires you to actually make a choice. While all choices are decisions, not every decision requires a choice – and it's choices that we struggle with, because they require us to commit to a particular course of action, and to sacrifice the different option.

In this case, we are being asked to weigh up all of this in fiendishly tough circumstances: there's a pressing time imperative and we simply haven't got enough knowledge for it to become clear which is the 'better' option. In other words, we're being asked to make this decision 'blind', because we simply can't know all the information we really need in order to make it. And yet the gravest possible consequences are at stake: the life of a child, the life of a firefighter who's also a father and the life of a volunteer who'll be taking in the pedal cutters. Their lives depend on what you're going to decide to do next.

What Is a Decision?

The two of us have spent our entire careers – nearly half a century between us – researching the processes by which individuals make decisions. Specifically, we are what you would call 'field psychologists' insofar as much of our work is in the field and working with real people (police, army, navy, air force, security, paramedics, interrogators) making real decisions. We don't just study students in the laboratory, we focus on real-time, high-stakes choices in the real world. We've studied the sorts of decisions human beings make in extremis, and we've studied what factors come into play when they make them. At the heart of our work is a desire to use our knowledge to help people make decisions more effectively.

Let's start by pinning down what a decision actually is. In our business, it's defined as 'a commitment to a course of action that is taken in order to achieve a desired goal'.[1] Looking at this definition, there are several important aspects that are critical to thinking about how you make decisions in life. The most important, as we expand on below, is that decisions involve actions *being taken*. This is a common misconception. Consider for a moment one of the questions we most enjoy putting to clients on our courses:

'Five frogs are sitting on a log. Four decide to jump off. How many are left?'

Answer: Five.

Why? Because there's a world of difference between 'deciding' and 'doing'.

When it comes to decision-making, many people focus on the process of choosing, often at the cost of remembering that a decision only becomes complete once it has been implemented in the real world.

What this means is that you can *decide* what you *want* to do all day long – you have decided that you *want* to get a new job, you *want* a new relationship, you *want* to propose to your long-term partner. But the decision has not been made until you have actually done it. To use a common motivational phrase, you have to *'do the damn thing'*. This is why in this book, while we focus on the process of helping you choose *what you want to do*, we know that this is only half the battle and to fully make life-changing decisions, you have to implement your intention.

There are three crucial words we'll come back to time and again throughout this book:

1. Commitment: Making sure that you are firmly committed and not still dithering about options.

2. Action: Not just thinking about what you will do but actually doing it.

3. Goal: Ensuring that you know what the point is and being clear about the goal you want to achieve. The more

precise the better – so instead of 'being more happy', try 'to enjoy at least five hours more free time in an average working week'.

We don't want you to become that frog stuck on the log. Deciding, but not doing.

How Do We Decide?

Before we explain how we conceptualise decisions, let's delve into the research. How have theories on decision-making developed over the years? Where are we now in terms of academic theories? What's the new thinking people like us have contributed to? And, critically, out of that research, which bits are going to be most useful to you?

If we go back to the beginning, scientists have been formally studying how we make decisions since the eighteenth century, and the first model to emerge from academia was called the classical model. It holds that people make choices based simply on what they assume will be the most favourable outcome.

Take, for example, the decision to buy a house, a car, a new kitchen or an expensive outfit for a big event. Here, you will be juggling with several different criteria. If you want to buy a car, for example, you may look at numbers of seats, price, fuel economy and insurance costs. All of these things are easy to find out with a little searching and can be compared. Furthermore, in this situation, it is easy to identify the 'best' decision as the one that has the highest evaluation across all variables. We can also easily identify 'errors' as any choice that has a 'lower score' than an alternative that was available to the decision maker at that time. Decisions have known outcomes, known values, and therefore we can 'know' what is good and what is bad.

Taking this one step further, we can add a degree of subjectivity to this process. Subjectivity is the idea that not all people may experience, feel or act in the same way – there can be a degree of *subjective* rationality (i.e. what is good for you, may not be good for me) and *temporal* rationality (i.e. what is a good decision at one time, may not be a good idea later). For example, Neil purchased a Ford Mustang, drawn to it because he was young and living in America; this was not an erroneous decision in July – it was an amazing car to drive around in the Boston summertime. But when December hit, and there was a foot of snow outside, he could not get his car out of the drive for two weeks.

Sounds simple, doesn't it? And logical. This is why we so often hold the assumption of rationality; the idea that we, and those around us, are rationally weighing up all courses of action before deciding. Interestingly, it's the same basis that's used to this day for the decisions made by some of the people we most often work with. In our own work, in fact, we often have to overcome the base assumption that decision makers are not only rational, but that they engage in a rational comparative process when making decisions. All too often we assume that a rational individual goes through a rational process of option evaluation and chooses (rationally) the best possible course of action for them.

The problem with the rational actor model is that it requires you to know the outcome of a decision before it is made. Which, while it might work when choosing a car, a house or a new kitchen, is not such an obvious key when it comes to many of the biggest decisions we make in life. Think about the dilemmas you have had in front of you over the past days or weeks. In many cases you know what will happen when you make your choice. But it is also likely that there are a few, more fiendish decisions in which you don't know what will happen. These fiendish decisions are often the most important, might involve other people, and probably are the ones you found (or are still finding!) the most difficult. Does that sound correct to you?

One of the reasons why the rational view of human decision-making has persisted is because the traditional model of testing decision-making has taken place 'in the laboratory'. Academics have tended to design experiments that *require* players to be logical. But as the study of decision-making developed, it became clear that psychologists were focusing on quite specific sorts of situations: ones in which the required information about outcomes was known or where there was little uncertainty. In other words, the situations psychologists were studying were very controlled, and so removed from the realities of life. They were the easy decisions! What makes your real-life decisions difficult are precisely the elements that textbooks have overlooked: time pressure; uncertainty; ill-defined goals; high personal stakes; fluid and dynamic changes to the information; and high accountability if anything goes wrong. And in these truer-to-life situations, the thing that was clearest to understand wasn't how people made their decisions, it was how they didn't do it.

As the US psychologist Gary Klein, who pioneered the study of decision-making in the real world, puts it, in our daily lives we don't come up with alternative options and don't compare them using the same methods of evaluation. Even when we do compare options, we don't make use of a specific system or set of techniques.[2] From this realisation, about the way human beings behave in the real world, a new model of decision-making began to emerge.

What mattered most, Klein argued, was not academic theories of how people *should* behave but rather how people *actually* behave in real-life settings, when faced with excruciating, or desperately hard, and potentially life-changing situations. In the trade, this became known as 'naturalistic decision-making' (NDM). Taking it a stage further, Klein made another important discovery: he studied high-octane decision makers (fire chiefs, police commanders, etc.) in real-life situations, and found that most size up a situation very quickly and come up with an option on how to proceed without even considering other choices.

How did that work? Klein put it down to what he tagged 'recognition-primed decision-making' (RPD). By studying real-life, edge-of-the-seat situations, he realised that expert decision makers rely on knowledge gleaned from many years of similar knife-edge moments. The more experienced an individual is in their field, the quicker and slicker they will be at opting for a particular course of action, because previous experience helps them identify what's happening and what's likely, on balance, to happen next. In effect, the phenomenon Klein identified mirrors the behaviour of chess grand masters. They don't need to consciously 'play out' moves, because they instinctively know, from years of experience, how a particular set of moves is likely to end.

RPD is based on the same kind of pattern recognition we see in elite sports performance. The same way elite sports players recognise patterns in the opposing team, expert decision makers look for patterns in their own environment that tell them what is the most likely thing to happen next. This often sets up the very simple decision rule: 'Did the action I took last time work?' If yes, do it again. If not, try something else.

We all do the same in our day-to-day life – we pick routes to work based on previous traffic jams we have encountered or we choose grocery stores based on previous experiences of whether they had that certain ingredient we were looking for. Experience is a vital asset, and one that often differentiates expert from novice performance precisely because they are able to use their immense 'library' of experiences to quickly identify what is going on and use previous decisions to help them calculate what they should do next.

We agree with Klein about the importance of experience, and that you should be aware of its significance in helping you guide your actions. But the problem we've realised you're likely to come up against is that many big life decisions are one-offs. You've never made a decision like whether to commit to a relationship with someone for life. You've never had to weigh up whether to move to a new city. You've never considered making a career change. So for these kinds of situations, we realised, you need a different sort of wisdom.

Least-Worst Decisions

Problems with decision-making are most acute when we face new, novel and unpredictable situations. Situations like the tunnel scenario; or the choice to change careers; or when we're diagnosed with a life-changing illness and have to make a decision over how it's treated. In these circumstances, as we have seen, every possible course of action involves the potential, or even the probability, of a negative, painful and/or tragic outcome. What's more, there are too many unknowns and too much volatility for previous experience to offer much in the way of learned wisdom or a 'rational' solution. These kinds of decisions challenge the way we have traditionally thought about decision-making; we cannot compare the outcomes of options because we do not know what exactly will happen and thus how we will feel about those outcomes – and nor do we have any previous experience to help us decide what we definitely should or should not do. In this sense, these decisions do not allow us to rationally select the most 'ideal' or even settle for the most 'workable' outcome.

Our way of explaining how you reach a decision in this sort of situation is in terms of a 'least-worst' choice: and we have spent a lot of our time as academics thinking about these least-worst decisions – the decisions we can truly call the hardest of all – and how to deal with them. In our training and academic work, we have defined least-worst decisions as those that involve multiple options, each of which has the potential to have a negative outcome, and in which your goal is to select the least-worst of the outcomes you face. Given that information is incomplete in a least-worst decision, and that it's not possible to second-guess what might happen next, how do expert decision makers move forward in these instances?

Let's look again at the tunnel scenario we outlined at the start of this chapter, knowing what we now know. We can start with the plea from the firefighter in the tunnel: if you remember, he is refusing to leave the young girl he is with until pedal cutters are brought in so he can cut her out of the wreckage. We have a binary decision: bring pedal cutters in or do not bring them in. Both possibilities have a best-case outcome and a worst-case outcome. The best-case scenario for not sending in a volunteer is there's no bomb, and eventually we save both the firefighter and the injured girl. A worse outcome, on the other hand, is that the bomb detonates, killing them both.

However, when we work it through, it's clear there's an even worse scenario, a worst possible outcome of all: which is that not only the eight-year-old girl, and the firefighter who won't leave her, but also a volunteer who's taken the pedal cutters into the tunnel, all die. That scenario can only happen if you decide to send a volunteer into the tunnel with the cutters: so, tempting though that course of action might be (after all, it also carries the biggest chance of success *if* there really is another bomb), it also carries the biggest risk of failure.

In other words, by not sending the pedal cutters into the tunnel, there is a possibility of both the child and the firefighter dying; but there's also a chance of them both surviving, if there's no bomb. And crucially, there is no risk of the worst-case outcome that could result if you decide to send someone else in with cutters. However – and this is why this decision is so difficult – deciding to avoid the worst-case scenario means that you are deciding to forgo the best-case scenario. It is this tension between trying to avoid the worst, while also hoping for the best, that makes least-worst decision-making so fiendishly hard.

The fact is this: the choice you're being asked to make requires a sacrifice. And making a sacrifice is one of the toughest things you'll ever have to do in your life.

Do You Have a Choice?

All this leads to another interesting point about decision-making, which is that the most seismic, or vital, or potentially catastrophic choices *may not be the hardest ones to make*. In our experience, people tend to assume that the bigger the consequences, the more difficult the decision. But more often it's having the freedom to choose between two courses of action, and indeed having to take accountability for the process of making a choice, that will cause you most difficulty. Take, for example, the following, military scenario:

In the summer of 2017, one of us (Neil) interviewed a US Lieutenant Colonel called Thomas Kellaway who commanded Special Operations Forces in Afghanistan in the months after the 9/11 attacks on his country. He was part of an offensive mission called 'Operation Enduring Freedom', which sought to track down and 'remove' Taliban forces. Kellaway described one of the most memorable decisions he made during that period.

His role was to manage air support: and on the night in question, there were five different special operations teams in the field, each one tracking a different target thought to possibly be Taliban. Suddenly, at almost exactly the same time, two of his teams reported an urgent need for air support. One team, made up of US soldiers, said gunshots were being fired at them; another team, made up of Germans, said they had been spotted by insurgents, and that these people were now circling their position and getting closer.

Kellaway only had one air squadron, and he had to decide which team to send it to.

Because the military has a very strictly agreed and pre-developed protocol to help staff make decisions, Lt. Col. Kellaway wasn't alone in the choice that faced him; in fact his decision was made for him. Kellaway knew he could only make a decision to send reinforcements if the squad on the ground were able to confirm their target was hostile: this is known in the trade as PID, or positive identification. For PID to be established, at least one of three criteria had to be met: the soldiers had to clearly see a uniform on their assailants, they had to be aware of open acts of hostility e.g. shooting or they had to know they were in a position of immediate threat. But when Kellaway questioned the US team, it quickly became clear they didn't have PID. They had seen muzzle flashes, but no one had been hit, their equipment hadn't been hit and they couldn't see any uniforms.

The concern, both for Kellaway and certainly for the team, was that despite the lack of these signals, the group they'd spotted were potentially dangerous. So Kellaway moved to the next protocol provided by the US Army, which states that if a team is compromised, its reaction should be to move away from the threat. 'I asked, do you have clear avenues of escape?' Kellaway remembered. 'Is there a reason you need to stay as close as you are?' There was not: so it was suddenly very clear what the team ought to do.

Meanwhile the German team were also concerned about the group they had encountered: they told Kellaway they believed at last 14 vehicles were moving towards them in a search pattern, that 'they know we are here and they are looking for us'. Once again, though, when Kellaway asked specifically whether they had established PID according to the criteria, they had to admit they had not. And so, again, he asked whether there was an escape route. And again, there was. As such, what looked like a really thorny decision was actually very easily resolved due to pre-existing protocols. However, if none of these protocols had been developed Kellaway would most certainly have been making some tough decisions.

Kellaway's story highlights what we might call the first rule of decision-making, and it is this: when faced with what seems like a decision, your initial task is to work out whether there is, in fact, a decision to be made at all. Sometimes in our lives, events conspire to present an illusion of a difficult choice, when in truth there is either no decision to be made or it's not actually our decision to make. For example, if a student were agonising over whether to take 3D art or textiles as a subsidiary of their course only to find that actually only one option was available, suddenly this is not a decision they need to agonise over anymore. We often find ourselves falling into this pattern of agonising of decisions that are not available to us, or that we do not have the power to make.

The Three Different Ways to Make a Decision

There's another way to look at all this, which we find helpful in identifying what *kind* of decision you are faced with and, indeed, what decision-making strategy you are going to be able to employ. This is referred to as the 'tri-modal model' of decision-making.

1. Follow the rules

First is to do what Kellaway did in the decision above: you 'match' what you *can do* with what you *should do* in this situation (according to pre-designed rules). So, for the military commander, when there is no PID it's clear they should not provide air support. This is doctrine, and it's why rules and regulations exist: they answer the question 'What should I do?' for you, so that you don't have to decide for yourself. You will have learned to make these decisions in your own life in the form of organisational policy. Often an organisation seeks to dictate how their employees should react in certain predictable situations by developing doctrine, standard operating procedures or even social and cultural norms. The goal here is to stop you from needing to think 'Should I do X or Y?' and instead think 'What would anyone who holds my position do in this situation?' You're sure to recognise this kind of thinking in your own life – you are often taught it in training and through a large number of organisational policy and procedure documents. They are making sure that when you face decisions in the workplace you (1) don't have to 'choose' how to react and (2) react in the way that best serves the organisation. In effect, the organisation has made that choice for you, long before you will ever have to.

2. Learn from past experience

We can view this mode of decision-making as RPD: your experience of similar decisions, in relatable situations, can help you make the decision you're currently facing. For example, imagine there was no doctrine for the situation Kellaway was facing, but that he didn't approve of giving air support unless he could guarantee there would be no civilian casualties because (let's speculate) he had seen this go wrong in the past. The decision he reaches is the same, but the journey to that decision, instead of hanging on an external policy, will be reached via prior experience.

What is critical is that you decide what to do based on your experience of facing a similar situation in the past and what happened. This view of decisions as being made by 'analogies' is widely used. As a parent, for example, you might decide on a course of action over an issue to do with your teenager because of what happened the last time you took that route out of this particular problem with their older sibling. And despite the seeming simplicity of making decisions based on 'what happened last time?', we shouldn't minimise the importance of this strategy. Making decisions based on analogies is shown to predict parenting decisions just as effectively as whether a US president decides to go to war.[3]

3. Make a choice

This is the form of decision-making we are most focused on in this book. It begins with the commitment to *choose* one course of action and centres on the question: 'Which of these options is the best means to my ends?' Psychologists such as Cohen and Lipshitz, who proposed the tri-modal theory of decision-making, argue that decisions require actual choice when:[4]

1. The environment presents multiple options.

2. An external pressure (organisational or cultural) requires you to justify your action by comparing it to another option.

3. The goals of the decision maker compete with one another, and advantages and disadvantages must be traded off in order to approach optimality.

This tri-modal framework is helpful because it explains why, when conducting our own research, we came across the perplexing phenomenon that people who have served in positions of immense authority, in war or in the emergency services, often say that they 'did not usually make any decisions' while at work. Initially this was hard to reconcile, but what we realised they were saying was not that they did not make any decisions – they made many decisions daily – but that they never made *choices*. And again, this is not to minimise the decision-making process or the immense emotional turmoil that making decisions (via matching or RPD) can cause. It's not that the other sorts of decision-making don't involve conflict: they do or can, because you may be emotionally conflicted over, for example, leaving a lover who has had a relationship with someone else, despite knowing you have decided you can never live with this. At the same time, a police officer can know that they need to take offensive action to save people's lives, but can still be deeply affected by the action that they had to take. But choices add a further layer of conflict because not only do you have to make a call on what to do, you also have to actively reject the alternate reality that could have been brought to life if the (best) version of the other choice came to pass.

Think about this point yourself: in the last few weeks or months, you may have made a range of decisions, but how many times have you had to reject an equally appealing alternative? That is the difference between a decision and a choice.

The immense conflict this can cause should not be underestimated. One clinical psychologist who specialises in military trauma (referred to as post-traumatic stress disorder or PTSD, and more recently moral injury), told us she was 'well aware' of the toll these decisions took on her clients' psychological health. She called them 'shoulda, woulda, coulda' decisions because they leave people with agonising 'what if' questions about what might have happened if they'd taken a different route.[5]

In all likelihood you'll have experienced this in your own life. Maybe you split up with a partner who you felt was not right for you, only to spend days wondering about whether it might have been possible to find a way of making things work out after all. Or you changed your job, and despite generally loving it, after a particularly bad day, or drinks out with your old colleagues, you can't help imagining a world in which you had stayed in your old job, got a promotion and eventually made it all the way to CEO. Choice breeds conflict in knowing what to do: but making the choice breeds a world of 'what if' possibilities that can haunt us forever.

What we most fear is loss

Beyond the process of having to choose, this concept of having to lose something is what makes choice so difficult. Humans are instinctively averse to loss and research has found that worries about what we fear we will *lose*, rather than what we hope we will gain, are hugely significant.[6] That's because human beings have a tendency to stress about what we're *not* going to get, instead of about what we *are* getting. That's a phenomenon generally known as FOMO – fear of missing out. Even when we're doing something we value and enjoy, part of us is regretting the very opportunities we had to sacrifice in order to be where we are.

Psychologists have discovered that this desire to avoid loss is so strong that it's the most common reason for one of what we believe is the most dangerous pitfalls of all in decision-making: inertia. Because although many people worry about making the wrong decision, what we've realised is far more common is an inability to make a decision at all. The big danger is that, when faced with a major decision, because of a fear of losing something you may not even have, you'll stall. This is something we have all experienced, and it can manifest in several 'tendencies' that all have the same net outcome: we fail to make a decision. Some of the most notable manifestations of this stalling are:

- Ignoring the problem. You might put the difficulty out of your mind, or decide to minimise it and tell yourself you've got other/bigger things to worry about.
- Starting to think about the decision, and then stopping. This often happens when the choice seems overwhelming, and it feels as though the easy way out is to bat it on to someone else.

- Deciding on a course of action, but then delaying it (this is also known as implementation failure). You've made your choice but you're hanging back – possibly not confident enough to move forward. We hope this book will equip you with knowledge that will help you avoid this happening.

Perhaps as you read this you will have noticed that you, too, have engaged in a few of these, perhaps within the same decision. This is why inertia is such an important concept (and why it is so important that we help you identify and overcome it), because we can all fall victim to it and it can stop us from gaining what we want through fear of what we might lose. In the following chapters, we'll be looking at this in a lot more detail.

DECISION TIME TIPS

1. A decision is a commitment to a course of action to achieve a specific goal. Thinking about something is not the same as deciding. To decide you must commit to it and act on it. In order to move forward, ask yourself the following questions:

   - What are my goals here? What do I want to actually achieve?
   - If there are several goals, what is the most important one?

- What action or set of actions do I need to do to achieve that goal?
- What do I need to commit to in order to take action?

2. A critical decision is a potentially life-changing one. We are not talking about everyday decisions, but decisions that are rare or even unique, but that matter. They are most often the ones when you are at a crossroads and you could go down either path. Here is a checklist of the things that can make a critical decision difficult. If your answer to just a few of these is yes, chances are you are at that crossroads!

- Is it high stakes?
- Is it irreversible once you've gone one way? (i.e. if you go down path A are you committed to that path only?)
- Is the task ambiguous? (i.e. there is no specific protocol or policy book)
- Is the situation one you have rarely (if ever) faced before? (i.e. you have very little or no experience)
- Is it time-sensitive? (i.e. you can't wait forever and you sense something has to be done but it's hard to know by when)
- Does it impact on you and those you care about?
- Is it hard to predict the outcome?
- Do all the options look equally bad (or, indeed, equally good) and it's hard to pick between them?

- Are you likely to feel regret if something goes wrong?

3. What is the consequence of being at a critical crossroads? The most frequent negative impact is the natural temptation to stay where we are and pick neither path. The trouble with this is that we become inert, staring at the pathways ahead, but not moving forward along any of them.

CHAPTER 2

Decision Inertia

I T STARTED AS an afternoon of birthday fun, and it ended with an almost unbelievably tough decision, taken in the full glare of the world's media.

The date was 23 June 2018; the place Mae Sai in Chiang Rai province in Thailand. The occasion was Peerapat 'Night' Sompiangjai's seventeenth birthday and, to celebrate, he was out with his fellow footballers from the local youth team the Wild Boars, and their assistant coach Ekkapol Chantawong.

The boys, all aged between 11 and 16, were on bicycles, and they cycled to one of their favourite haunts – the Tham Luang cave complex, which lies below a mountain range on the border of Thailand and Myanmar. The system is 10km long and has many passages and tunnels; but the boys knew it well and often explored there.

The boys only intended to stay an hour or two, but several hours later they still hadn't returned home and their families were concerned. Some knew of the boys' plan to visit the cave. When their bikes were found, their relatives' fears were confirmed. The cave system is relatively safe during the dry season, but the rains had come and the cave had flooded. Unable to get out, the youngsters had had no alternative but to venture deeper, and they were now stranded, cut off by the flood, around 4km from the entrance.

For an agonising week the boys' families waited, as divers flew in from around the world to help with the search. And then, ten days after they had headed into the cave, the boys and their coach were found alive by two British divers, who could hardly believe they'd all survived in such difficult and harrowing circumstances: they were huddled on a ledge, had no food, and had been drinking water that was dripping down the cave walls.

But the jubilation was brief, because it was painfully obvious that the boys were far from safe, and that the greatest challenge lay ahead. Heavy rains were forecast in just a few days' time and subsequent flooding would cut off, and likely kill, the boys if they remained inside the cave. To keep them alive, divers were dispatched with supplies of food, blankets and oxygen tanks.

With the situation now critical, the head of the rescue mission, Narongsak Osotthanakorn, faced an almost unimaginably difficult decision – with the world's media straining for every detail. In essence, there were two choices: Osotthanakorn could leave the youngsters inside the cave until the end of the monsoon season, with divers providing food, water and air, or he could try to get them out quickly. Both options carried significant risk of death for the youngsters and their rescuers. What Osotthanakorn decided to do was to get the boys out: and to do that, he had them sedated and carried, on stretchers, through the maze of tunnels.

Over 100 divers, supported by 10,000 more people, took part in the nail-biting mission. Within three days all the boys, their coach and all the rescue team emerged unscathed. And minutes after the last person got out, the cave flooded again. It felt unbelievable: across Thailand people sounded car horns, clapped and cheered.

The operation had gone better than anyone had dared expect: once it was accomplished, it was easy to fete Osotthanakorn and the team, and to revel in how he made the 'right' decision. But as with all decisions, there was no 'right' decision at the time the choice to move in and start the rescue was made. What faced Osotthanakorn was, in effect, a myriad of factors that conspired to make his choice just about as difficult as it could be. Given that he would have to 'carry the can' for what happened, it was clear his reputation, career and entire future was on the line. Beyond the professional ramifications was a barrage of personal fears: who could live with themselves having made a choice that went on to take the lives not only of a group of young people, but potentially the lives of many rescuers as well?

What's fascinating about the Thai cave situation for us as psychologists studying decision-making is that it encapsulates many of the rabbit holes that can mitigate against making a good choice. The first of these is fear. Fear, as everyone knows, can be immobilising: we've all heard the phrase 'rooted to the spot with fear'. And the research is quite clear about the biggest fear associated with decision-making: the fear that we will go on to regret the decision; our biggest concern isn't making the 'wrong' decision, it's making a decision we'll later regret.[1] Of course, regret isn't just about what happens next after we've made the decision – it's about regret we might feel for alternative courses of action we might have chosen, other paths we might have pursued. From all this emerges another major issue that rears up time and again in the science of good decision-making: and that is, it requires bravery to overcome fear and commit to a decision. Let's examine all this in a bit more detail.

The Psychology of Doing Nothing

> A hungry donkey stands between two hay piles that are identical in every way. The donkey always chooses whichever hay is closest to him. Both piles are exactly the same distance apart, one on his right, one on his left. Which pile of hay will the donkey choose to eat?

The above paradox, originally proposed by Aristotle, was made famous by the French philosopher Jean Buridan, and has since been referred to as 'Buridan's ass'.[2] In this paradox the donkey is unable to choose between which of the two treats is more appealing, and will, in turn, starve to death in the paralysis of choice. I (Neil) recently decided to try out this paradigm with our puppy (a nine-month-old, 70lb golden retriever who loves all food), by giving him a treat, and then before he can chew it, offering him the exact same treat again. Regular as clockwork, he would drop the treat in his mouth, in order to grab the same treat out of my hand. I would then pick up the treat off the floor and offer it to him again, and repeat the process. My dog could go a full 120 seconds of taking treats without ever actually eating one of them. In my dog's mind, as with Buridan's ass, he cannot decide between the two equally appealing treats, and cannot bring himself to turn down one of the treats (or bales of hay), even though the process of not deciding means that he will never get any. I would recommend any dog-owning reader experiment with this trick to see just how easy it is to focus on what we could have, at the cost of what we currently have. Eventually though, and unlike when we make decisions, the dog gets both treats (because, of course, he is a very good boy).

This philosophical conundrum reflects a common observation that when people face equally attractive (or unattractive) choices they can become paralysed choosing between equal options. Many parents may have observed this behaviour when asking their child to decide what toy they want for their birthday, only to then observe them being unable to decide between the many toys that they want, leading to an inevitable disappointment in the toy they choose.

As psychologists we often find ourselves preoccupied with the study of behaviour – that is, studying what people do when they are presented with a situation or stimuli. What this means, however, is that we sometimes neglect to study those situations in which people do not take action. This is the psychology of doing nothing and, despite having far less attention, knowing when we do not act may be even more important than studying when we do.

Many people assume that the biggest 'mistake' you can make when making a decision is to choose the 'wrong' thing. But our experience and research has led us to believe something very different: the biggest 'mistake' you can make is to do nothing.

In decision-making, we can find ourselves inert for various reasons: through the lack of any motivation (i.e. you do not want to have to make a decision), the presence of two appealing choices pulling you towards them (i.e. two equally exciting offers, leaving you spoilt for choice) or the presence of two unappealing choices that push you away from them (e.g. having to choose a lunch date between two people who you very much don't want to eat with).

In fact, given all this, you could argue that whenever we're faced with making a decision, we're wired to want to decide to do nothing. Psychologists have even argued that inertia is a form of armour or self-protection, since our expectation seems to be that we will feel less regret about doing nothing than about doing something.[3] What the two of us believe is that we need to understand that and override it – because very often in our lives, doing nothing will make the situation worse, especially in the long term.

The Inertia Traps

One of the most important parts of taking our research 'outside of the laboratory' is that we can see in real time the many and complex ways that actions can fail to occur, even when it's plain as day to everybody that an action is required.

We have referred to this tendency as 'decision inertia' – the inability to commit to a course of action in time, or at all – and it manifests in a slowing down of the decision-making process. Looking around at some of the challenges facing us now, we can see inertia everywhere. We watched, in real time, as countries of the world failed to intervene in the 2011 Syrian civil war that led to the rise of the Islamic State; we watched countries fail to mobilise resources or lock down as news of the Covid-19 pandemic began to emerge from China. And we see, in the world around us, individuals who struggle to change their careers, relationships, living conditions, major degree programmes or behavioural habits even though they know that they should. All of these are examples of inertia, but while the end result is the same (an absence of action), there are many different ways in which an action can fail to materialise.

The idea that there are multiple and different paths to inaction was something that I (Laurence) first formalised working alongside PhD student Claudia van den Heuvel on a simulated terrorist attack in 2010.[4] Using an immersive simulation method (called HYDRA) in which police officers are able to navigate a complex evolving situation, receive real-time intelligence, ask for more information, and even chat with officers in other units, van den Heuvel, myself and director of HYDRA Jonathan Crego sought to explore what the processes of decision-making looked like as these police officers navigated extreme uncertainty. We used observations, video tapes of them doing the event, post-event debriefs and their own decision 'logs' (diary entries explaining their choices) to support our assessments.

What we found was that high levels of uncertainty were derailing the officers' ability to stick to the decision-making process, resulting in either non-actions (omitting the decision altogether) or apparent actions (actions that deferred the choices until later moments or passed them on to other agencies). Despite being well aware of the immense costs of delaying action, and the goal of making sure the police officers in this scenario saved as many civilian lives as possible, these behaviours were defined as 'derailments' from the 'save life' approach because, according to subject matter experts who reviewed their behaviour, the teams were not implementing critical decisions that they should have made in a timely manner, potentially culminating in detrimental consequences for the investigation. Studies like this have allowed us to outline three main ways that people fail to act, which we'll examine by way of an everyday example:

Hannah is a 58-year-old woman living in the UK. She's been married for 26 years and she's the mother of two children aged 22 and 25.

Hannah's marriage has never been entirely 'happy', but like most marriages it's had its good times and its bad. It would be true to say, though, that Hannah has had doubts about the wisdom of having married Simon almost since their honeymoon. The couple married quickly, after discovering that their eldest child was on her way; if it hadn't been for the pregnancy, Hannah doubts she'd have ever married Simon at all. The pair have very different backgrounds and, as their marriage has played out, they've realised, time and again, that they have different priorities about how they spend their time and money, and what they most value and care about.

Nevertheless, like many couples, they've cobbled things together across more than two decades. Both Hannah and Simon are very close to their children, although they see what they need to offer as parents differently. For Hannah it's primarily about emotional warmth and security, while for Simon it's about having enough money to support them and helping them get on to the career ladder. Now, though, their kids have moved out of the family home and are living their own lives – and, for Hannah, that's put her relationship with Simon into close focus.

For Simon, things are absolutely fine as they are. He tends to focus more on his work (he runs a chain of garages) than on his family life. As far as he's concerned, marriage to Hannah, who's an HR manager, is 'good enough', and he's never going to rock the boat to end it. Nor, though, is he willing to take up Hannah's suggestion that they should go for relationship counselling as a way of improving things. Basically, he's not a conciliator and, as far as he's concerned there's nothing that needs fixing in his marriage.

For Hannah, though, there's been a fear worrying away at the back of her mind for many years now that she could be happier with someone else – or even on her own. She feels she's been squashed and bullied in her marriage to Simon, and that the marriage has been very much on his terms. She knows though that she'll face huge upheaval if she decides to leave Simon – and also that her children may well side with him and accuse her of breaking up their family.

For a couple of years now she's been ruminating on whether she ought to leave or not. Because deciding to separate is a huge and terrifying decision, and she knows it could leave her lonely into her sixties and seventies. But on the other hand, she's not getting any happier in her relationship with Simon, and she's stopped believing things will ever improve.

Decision avoidance

Decision avoidance may be one of the most common methods of failing to make a decision. It constitutes the many ways in which we avoid thinking about a problem. It is cognitively light and involves no effort; we simply push the doubts to the back of our mind and focus our attention and energy on something else. In Hannah's case, the first two decades of her marriage were a time when it was very easy to avoid thinking about her marriage. The chaos and strain of being two working parents, with two growing children, didn't give her a lot of time to think about any underlying problems or feelings she was having, and made it very easy to convince herself that now 'was not the time' to be thinking about this decision.

With decision avoidance, we instinctively double down to convince ourselves that what we are doing is right rather than embracing the possibility that our behaviour is wrong.

Psychologists have long identified this as the 'sunk costs' tendency: what it means is that, despite the fact that a course of action is no longer meeting our expectations, we continue to sink time and money into it rather than consider the possibility that we need to change. So, we finish bad meals; we stay in bad relationships; we wear expensive clothes we bought but don't like; we renovate houses we bought on an impulse. If you recognise yourself in any of this, chances are you're avoiding facing the possibility that you may need to make a decision.[5] Furthermore, to embrace the possibility that we need to make a decision might be to tacitly acknowledge that we were wrong in the first place. And that's something else we are naturally not inclined to do.[6]

The fact is, almost all of us have avoided making a decision at one time or another in our lives, but if it becomes a habit, or if you're doing it to avoid a pivotal life change that you know makes sense, it's something you need to address.

Do you regularly find yourself trying to distract yourself from something that's bothering you underneath? Do you say or think things like, 'I'll make myself think about something else' or 'I'll leave this to think about later'? Or do the words 'It's easier to keep things as they are than to change everything' float through your mind from time to time? Added to which, do you push these thoughts to the back of your mind to avoid having to embrace the possibility that you were not right in the first place, or that a path you are currently on has not turned into what you thought it might be? If this is you, it's worth taking time to properly explore what's going on. We talk about the importance of knowing when to change in the later chapters of this book. But avoiding even thinking about *if* you have to change is a common form of inertia.

Redundant deliberation

The second form of decision inertia is demanding and effortful – it distracts you, fills your mind with worry and 'what ifs', and absorbs countless hours of your (and your friends' and loved ones') time while you try to work out what you should do. Hannah has a few close girlfriends, and she spends a lot of time talking with them about her feelings about Simon and their marriage, and her conundrum over whether to leave him. There's always lots to ruminate on – always a new chapter to the story that they can unpack and plenty to chew over in terms of what Simon does and doesn't do, ways in which he's incredibly frustrating and ways in which he's a good father to their kids.

However, Hannah has been rehearsing these arguments with her friends for at least the last five years and there's clearly a danger that she'll just carry on and on, blowing this way and that about whether to leave Simon or not, and never getting round to a decision. And that's quite different from making a positive decision to stay with him. What's more, all the endless focus on her marriage and Simon's place in her life is stalling her chances of working out what she wants for her life; marriage, even a good one, is only part of what makes us the human beings we want to be. With her endless procrastination Hannah is allowing her marriage to take up too much of her, while failing to reach a conclusion about where she wants it to fit into her life moving forward.

What we've discovered in our research is that the most frequent and dangerous form of decision inertia is, like Buridan's ass and Hannah's marriage, overthinking a problem and still being unable to decide.[7] We call this specific sort of decision inertia 'redundant deliberation', and we define it as 'perpetual rumination over the outcomes of a choice for no added gain, leading to not acting in time or not acting at all'. And, unlike maintaining the status quo by avoiding thinking about the problem (for example, with Hannah, this would take the form of, 'I don't even want to think about this problem, I'm sure it's fine, let's talk about something else'), redundant deliberation is cognitively extremely demanding. For Hannah, redundant deliberation might look like this:

> I don't want to leave him, he's a great father, but on the other hand, it's making me so unhappy. I think that is really starting to impact on my relationship with the children. But, maybe I can improve that or work on it. But then again, for how much longer? But then again, maybe I'm being too self-focused. Sarah, Chloe, what do you think?

And so on . . .

Redundant deliberation is all about overthinking a problem and, what's worse, it's often obsessive. Hannah is engaged in a constant loop of talking to her friends about what to do about her marriage to Simon, hoping that in every fresh conversation there will be some golden moment when she'll suddenly be able to see the way that lies ahead. With redundant deliberation, we ruminate obsessively about possible future outcomes and 'what ifs' to the point that the time we spend wondering means the situation has now moved on. In Hannah's case, it may reach a point where leaving Simon is no longer viable as she gets older and forging a new life for herself gets harder and harder.

Quite probably you'll have observed behaviour like this around you in your own life. How many times have you listened to a friend, or colleague, deliberate over a problem? The contents of the calculation may change day by day, week by week, month by month. They may even come to a different decision each time ('Right, I'm staying', 'Right, I've had enough, I'm leaving'), but the outcome remains the same: no decision is ever made. This is why redundant deliberation is so appealing, and indeed so easy to fall victim to. It is the illusion of progress without ever getting any closer to the deadline. Deliberating without arriving at a solution is simply running as fast as you can to stay in the same place.

Take a moment to think about issues around redundant deliberation in your own life. If you obsessively ruminate over what could be, and spend time thinking about what it will look like and feel like if you choose path A over path B, or if you're constantly trying to find out more information about the pathway you could embark on, the chances are you're experiencing this phenomenon yourself. It takes up a lot of your energy, so it's going to feel very fatiguing. You need to be self-aware to identify it – and then you need to be strong enough to admit that no more information is going to help, and that you're done with deliberating. And act.

Implementation failure

There's a third and final form of inertia: we call it implementation failure, and it means that a decision is made, but not acted upon. In other words, an individual or group assesses a situation, develops a plan and agrees on how it will be executed, but they don't follow it through.

It's easy to imagine that happening with Hannah: having spent so long mulling over whether to go or whether to stay with Simon, she eventually decides to go – but doesn't take the essential next step of working out practically how she will do this, as well as how she's going to handle it with Simon and their children emotionally.

The simple fact is that for a decision to be meaningful, it must be acted on. For example, say you're a parent concerned about your children's screen time. You have a chat about it as a family and agree that Sunday mornings will be screen-free. Everyone in the family agrees on what's been decided, but you may need to check that everyone is sticking to the plan (and that probably includes the parents!).

Or at work, if you're working in a team – and particularly if you're heading a team – you need to check that a plan has been acted on in the way you wanted it acted on, otherwise you'll have made no impact. Going back to our example of Hannah, implementation failure constitutes what may seem like an immeasurable gap between deciding to leave her husband and actually packing her bags (or having him pack his bags) to actually go. It may be the hardest step in the process, because implementing a decision makes it harder to reverse. Changing one's mind is easy enough – we do it every day, every hour – but implementing an action (even if it is reversible) takes time and creates hesitancy to act when we are unsure.

Implementation failure is widespread because it is in the gap between deciding and doing that our levels of perceived stress are highest. The greatest level of stress for a parachute jumper is not when they are on the plane, or when they have jumped, but when they have decided to jump but could still back out.[8] It is in the gap between deciding and doing, the last hurdle in decision-making, that we are at our most vulnerable to fail to act.

Take a moment now to think about a challenging decision you have faced in the past, or even one you expect to face. Can you see yourself falling into these traps? Did you avoid the problem? Did you become absorbed in the process of trying to decide? Or did you know, deep down, what you wanted to do, but failed to do it (in time, or at all?). Often we find that knowing what the inertia traps are, and being able to identify them, can be enough to help people overcome doubt and commit to making a decision.

This is why the case of the Thai cave rescue is so impressive. It would have been easy and, indeed, understandable if Osotthanakorn had fallen into the trap of holding off from making a decision. Not only were there crucial unknowns in the range of possibilities he was looking at (whether there might be another way into, and out of, the cave; whether the boys could be brought out alive by divers), he was also under intense scrutiny and would have known that every element of his thought process would be agonised over endlessly afterwards. Plus, and most crucially of all, there were many lives at risk: 13 lives already in danger, and many more who would be put at risk by a rescue operation. The fact that Osotthanakorn didn't prevaricate allowed the way forward that led to all the lives being saved. Only movement, only action, can lead to a situation being improved. Whatever risks it brings, there are also risks in remaining static: if Osotthanakorn had not acted when he did, all the lives inside the cave would have been lost when it eventually flooded.

Look at the decisions of those around you who you admire – perhaps they took a chance on love and lived happily ever after; perhaps they dropped out of high school and started a business, and it is now a huge success. Look at the decisions you have made that you are most proud of, or perhaps least proud of. In many cases, the people we admire, and specifically the decisions that made them, are those in which it would have been *easier to become inert*. But instead of avoiding, deliberating or failing to implement, they acted. This is why we admire them, and why the costs of inaction are often so high; it often stands in the way of us achieving our potential.

Inaction on a Wider Scale

In political leadership, as in Hannah's marriage, needlessly protracted decision-making can be costly and damaging. Allowing a situation to evolve beyond the capacity to deal with it can cost both money and lives. For example, in the Haiti earthquake of 2010, which resulted in 250,000 deaths, agencies were criticised for being too slow due to weak humanitarian leadership and poor prioritisation of relevant information.[9] During a period of heavy flooding in the UK in 2012, which ended up costing more than £600 million, criticism was directed at uncertainty of roles and responsibilities and a lack of leadership.[10] In these cases the responses were not viewed negatively for people making *the wrong decisions*, but not making *any decisions quick enough*.

And then, of course, there's the Covid-19 pandemic. In the years ahead, many governments are going to be criticised for being slow to act – as German Chancellor Angela Merkel said, the virus punishes half measures.[11] At the beginning of the pandemic there was almost a perfect storm in decision-making terms. Making choices was delayed because all the options looked (and indeed were) very bad indeed: either you close down the country's economy or many people are going to die. And in this pandemic there was no operating procedure or experience to fall back on: the last pandemic of this magnitude was a century ago. What's more, the stakes were extraordinarily high – and the path ahead exceptionally unclear. And in all these circumstances, the single most common problem we have identified in decision makers – a failure to act in time or even at all – was the result we saw, time and again. What we have argued for many years, and what Covid-19 unfortunately demonstrates for all to see, is that decision inertia is more problematic than decision error in critical situations. Much of the time, it isn't doing the *wrong* thing that causes catastrophe, it's *failing to do anything at all*.

So how can we break this inertia and overcome our inbuilt tendency to keep the status quo, and forge a new path into the unknown? In the next chapter, we're going to help you to look within to identify how you can initiate the actions you want in your life – whatever they may be. We'll explore who you really are, what your values are and what you want the world to be, because the most important part of overcoming inertia is knowing who we are, how we feel and what we want.

DECISION TIME TIPS

1. Do not avoid thinking about a decision because you are scared about what it might mean if you do think about it. You can still decide that you are right where you need to be, but if you avoid thinking about it you will never know if you really need to change.

2. If you have a major issue bubbling away somewhere in the back of your mind, and you keep putting off thinking about it, set yourself a timetable to address it which is achievable and reasonable – and then stick to it.

3. If you've identified redundant deliberation, you need to reflect on the key goals in your life in order to

---

move forward. Focus not on the best (unrealistic) option, but instead on the least-worst one, and you're in business to make the change you've been sitting on. Ask yourself whether you've taken the necessary steps to do what you want to do or whether you've just formulated a goal and not yet put any plans into action. If that's you, you're stuck at the crossroads – to move on, write down a basic checklist of the actions you need to take and cross each one off as you execute them.

4. Least-worst first. In order to push past an inertia trap you may need to sacrifice something. In some cases that might mean forgoing one good option for an even better one (you can't have your cake and eat it); in other cases it's about tolerating the least worst of two options (option A is bad and we want to avoid it, but option B is worse and we must avoid it). Sometimes you can create a third option that didn't readily seem apparent and which is actually a good outcome, but when there really are only bad outcomes you may need to evaluate which is the least worst.

CHAPTER 3

Know Thyself

AMELIA WAS ALREADY in her hospital gown, waiting to be wheeled down to theatre, when she made her decision: she wasn't going to have this operation. Yes, she had breast cancer, but no, a double mastectomy wasn't for her. There was going to have to be another way to sort out the problem.

It was a seismic choice, but Amelia hadn't reached it on her own: her surgeon understood that decisions around healthcare, while sometimes viewed in wholly 'scientific' terms, are in fact some of the most holistic decisions we ever take. While on paper the 'best' way of dealing with Amelia's cancer was to remove her breasts, in practice, what Amelia and her surgeon had realised was that the risk to Amelia's sense of self, and her mental health, outweighed the benefits of going ahead with the surgery.

Instead, Amelia's surgeon agreed to go ahead with a lumpectomy to remove just the cancer, which was followed up with radiotherapy.

How, then, did it take until the eleventh hour for Amelia to make her choice? Looking back, she says, she can see that she failed to realise, early on, that she actually had a choice. To make a decision, you have to realise there is a decision available to make. Initially, Amelia had been so terrified about having cancer that she'd thought she had to go along with whatever the oncology team recommended. It was only in the discussion she had with her surgeon on the day the operation was planned that she realised there might be another option.

As we've seen, working out whether a decision is possible is vital – and especially when it comes to health, that often means asking a lot of questions, including the one Amelia omitted to articulate: 'I understand that what you're recommending is the safest possible way, and perhaps it's the way most women would want to go, but is there another way that might suit me better?'

Once she'd established – albeit at the last minute – that a decision was possible, Amelia was able to draw down very quickly on what she needed to know to make her choice. 'I'd known for a long time that who I am is very bound up in my breasts,' she explains. 'Their loss, for me, would be tremendous – and when I finally got to tell my doctor how I felt, she agreed that we definitely shouldn't go ahead with what would be a completely irreversible, and life-changing, operation.'

Although it was an enormous decision, Amelia discovered it was also an easy one, in the final analysis, to make. 'I've got a very clear sense of what matters to me, and I was able to call on that,' she says. 'My family are absolutely the most important thing in my life: so if opting to keep my breasts had involved a risk to my life, especially a significant one, I wouldn't have gone down this route. But once it was clear that my cancer was unlikely to kill me, I was able to think about my own sense of who I am and what matters to me. I knew that I would be able to preserve my sense of myself best by doing the minimum, physically speaking, and that even if that brought risks of a recurrence, it would be less of a problem for me.' Seven years on, her cancer has not returned and Amelia says even if it does in the future, she knows she will never regret the choice she made.

What was critical to Amelia in making this decision was knowing, without doubt, who she was and what was important to her. Knowing ourselves is critical to effective decision-making and it involves answering several questions: how am I feeling in the moment, who am I as a person and what is the most important thing to me in the situation? While these questions sound easy to answer, we are often not as good at answering them as we think, and if we do not know ourselves well enough, we run the risk of making decisions for the wrong reasons, leading to regret. Let's look at this in more detail.

How Do I Feel?

In the summer of 2012, the Metropolitan Police were gearing up for the London Olympics. Over 471,000 people were expected to come to the United Kingdom from across the world to watch over 10,500 athletes from 204 countries compete in a range of sporting events. It was going to be a hot (by British standards) summer, and the security effort going on behind the scenes was immense.

One big concern for the authorities was the risk of terrorist attacks on the underground that would be packed with fans travelling between the different London Olympic sites. This was viewed as especially high-risk given that in 2005 London had been brought to a standstill after four suicide bombers detonated improvised explosive devices on three underground trains and one bus, killing 52 and injuring more than 700. Underground trains have often been popular targets for terrorist attacks since they are densely populated and cannot use airport-style security. This, coupled with the media attraction of the Olympics, made the perceived threat of a terrorist attack higher than usual (at the time the United Kingdom terror alert level was already 'substantial'). One of the mitigation strategies used by the Metropolitan Police was to have extra police officers patrolling the underground trains during peak hours.

As part of the training programme for these officers, we were asked to facilitate a course on decision-making under conditions of stress. The message was simple: it was not about the complexities of how to 'profile' a potential terrorist, but rather about the pressures that being underground on the train would place on the officers, and the effect this would have on their decision-making. We did a simple exercise, in which we drew an empty brain on a white board and asked them what stresses they expected they'd be under while patrolling. 'It's going to be hot,' one officer suggested. So we filled in a bit of the brain. 'We are wearing heavy protective gear,' another said. We filled in a bit more of the brain. 'I'll be exhausted after twelve hours on my feet,' another volunteered from the back of the room. We filled in a bit more of the brain. 'I'll probably be starving hungry,' yelled a slightly more jaded officer. Again, we filled in a bit more of the brain. After a few more stressors and strains were collected, we took a step back and looked at what we had drawn. Our empty brain was now almost full with colour blocks representing the strain they'd be under. 'Now, with all that already going on,' we asked them, 'what space do you think you'll have left to make a complicated decision?'

There's a big phenomenon here that too many of us overlook: because our bodies and our minds are so closely intertwined, the stresses and strains on our bodies put boundaries on the ability and agility of our minds to function.

The most acute version of this is what we call the 'fight or flight response'. It's defined as the 'immediate physiological reaction that occurs when danger or a threat to survival is perceived by an organism'.[1] In the words of one of our colleagues in the US, it can be summarised as follows: when you're up against it, you become 'fast, strong and dumb'.

Evolution didn't prime our bodies for efficient decision-making in the twenty-first century. In fact, we have evolved in a way that directly hampers the kind of decision-making we're discussing in this book. Big decisions can feel scary, and scary triggers 'fight or flight', but the physical responses associated with that aren't helpful – they route our blood *away* from our brains, and that makes it harder to reach a decision. The brain is an organ and, to work, it needs blood; the more work it needs to do, the more blood is required.

That's why psychological brain research – for example, a brain MRI scan – measures the flow of blood to the brain cells, to assess neural activity.

The fight or flight response is one way blood can be diverted from the brain, but there are others. Sleep deprivation, hunger and physical exercise all have the same effect. Sleep deprivation has been found to strongly impair human functioning: research shows that people who operate for long periods of time without sleep are slower to react, make more errors, have trouble recalling stored information and are less able to maintain attention.[2] Tired people also show decreased activity and flexibility as well as difficulties generating new ideas or solutions. Other research, using MRI scans, found that individuals who had been sleep deprived for 24 hours had reduced blood oxygenation in areas of the frontal and parietal lobes of the brain – areas that we know are critical for action planning and decision-making.[3] The frontal lobe of the brain integrates motivation, emotion, somatosensory information and external sensory information to create unified, goal-directed action. It's at the top of the hierarchy of neural structures devoted to the ways we respond to events and decide what to do. It's crucial to decision-making: if its processes are impaired in some way, we aren't going to be able to make decisions effectively, especially those least-worst decisions that we know make the biggest demands on our cognitive abilities.

In one study we are particularly fond of citing, a group of sleep-deprived soldiers were conducting a training mission in which they were meant to fire live ammunition at a group of stationary targets.[4] However, the researchers swapped out their live ammunition for blanks and swapped the 'stationary' targets for real, and very much moving, people. So when the cadets were given the order to fire what they thought were real lethal bullets, the targets that were meant to be cardboard cut-outs started moving.

What do you think happened? Did the soldiers panic, drop their guns, shriek in horror at how close they had come to murdering random civilians? Well, no. Sixty per cent of those in the exercise continued to shoot at the live targets despite them moving; and of the 40 per cent who did notice they were real people and decided not to shoot, only one individual warned the others. The researchers noted that lack of sleep and severe stress reduce cognitive abilities, which play a key role in decision-making. It is possible that some of the students who took part in the research were hallucinating because of their own sleep deprivation.

Hunger has the same effect; so, too, does physical exertion. All these issues – sleep, hunger and physical exertion – are big factors in military decision-making, since soldiers often have to make life-or-death decisions while yomping around unfamiliar territory, having had neither enough food or sleep. There's what we could call an *arms race* for energy within the body – and anything that lowers the overall amount of energy available for the brain, reduces the resources available to make hard choices. Now, while we (hopefully) only experience the fight or flight response rarely, even in milder form it can lower the resources available to the brain for functioning (think of how you feel after you've seen a scary movie). And at the same time, sleep deprivation, hunger and physical exercise all move blood away from the parts of the brain involved in complex cognitive processing and towards other, at that time perceived as more needy, parts of the body. You'll have experienced this for yourself: for example, if something scares you, you may well feel butterflies in your stomach – this is the blood rushing away from your stomach (digestion being less important than avoiding being digested). And if you've ever had to brake suddenly because the car in front unexpectedly comes to a halt, you have avoided an accident with your quick thinking, but you've perhaps felt the changes in your body as blood rushed to your legs and away from your brain (and also your stomach – hence the butterflies); that's your evolutionary self preparing you to make a getaway the old-fashioned way.

Scientists are still only just beginning to understand the tumultuous effects of the body on the mind, so it's perhaps not surprising that how soldiers, police officers and even astronauts handle the immense physiological pressures of their environments and make effective decisions is still an emerging area of psychological research. But the implications for your everyday life are clear – and you can consider them as either chronic strain or acute strain.

Acute strain

Acute strain is a moment of immense emotional reaction that primes your body with a fight or flight response. Perhaps you've just been told you're being 'let go' from work, or you have found out your partner is having an affair, or your best friend has betrayed a confidence. How might these moments make you feel physically? Now think about the biological processes that are causing these feelings: it's likely you're feeling butterflies, blood is rushing to your muscles or your legs feel weak. Your emotional brain is now driving the ship. In such instances, if you're facing a decision that could have long-lasting consequences (should you launch into a tirade against your employer? Tell your partner you're leaving them? Tell your best friend you'll never speak to them again?), this is the moment for a deep breath. You need to let your body calm down and come back to the problem when your mind can fully engage with all the dimensions of what's going on.

One way to do this is to use distraction. You can have a 'go-to' mantra that you repeat in your mind (for example, a nursery rhyme or tongue twister). Distraction is a good way to take you out of a rapidly escalating sense of anxiety. Another is breathing – put a hand up to your mouth, then gently breathe out, then in, then a longer breath out. Repeat three times. If you are getting really anxious, another option is to walk around if you can – this gets blood flowing and can also help you calm down.

It's important to give yourself time: time for your body to be back in a more optimal state, time to have thought through what's going to happen next. Most of the life decisions we're addressing in this book aren't instant decisions: they're not something you have to decide in the moment. It's not like swerving to avoid a child in the road when you're driving. There is a reason that legally there is a difference between a murder in the heat of the moment – the man who stabs his partner's lover at the moment he discovers them together – and murder in the first degree – the partner who·drives home, gets a weapon and returns. The latter had a chance to *think* and *reason*.

Chronic strain

One of the popular trends at the moment is the ability to track our physiological health – we're talking about devices such as smartphone health apps and activity trackers. Tracking the health of our body has led to a greater understanding of the many drains on how our body is feeling. One company, which allows people to track their daily 'recovery' score, therefore allowing us to see precisely what, in our everyday life, drains the body's ability to function, has identified three main sources of health drains:[5]

1. physical (working out with high volume, and high intensity, with poor balance between rest and working out)

2. lifestyle (diet and nutrition, alcohol, sleep habits and stress)

3. biological factors (age, gender and any chronic health conditions)

If these factors affect our body's ability to recover, they will also affect our mind's ability to operate under stress and complexity. Have you ever taken an exam while hungover? Have you articulated your emotions or tried to handle a disagreement after a long day at work or a stressful commute?

In these situations your body is under strain, and that strain is taking up your resources and hindering your ability to make complicated decisions.

To put this point in perspective, we recently conducted a study in which we asked people to make immensely complicated least-worst decisions.[6] However, before they made the decisions, half of the individuals were given a three-minute mindfulness breathing exercise that allowed them to calm themselves and focus on controlling their emotions. The other half listened to an audiobook excerpt. Those who were asked to breathe and think about how they felt were more approach-orientated – they wanted to make a more positive impact on the situation, rather than being cautious and worrying about doing the wrong thing. They were also faster to assess the situation and choose their course of action. Three minutes of breathing was all it took for someone to not only feel completely different, but act completely differently. We have put the script for this activity in the appendix (page 225). Perhaps next time you face a particularly challenging situation, or can feel yourself getting stressed and overwhelmed, you can try it. See it if helps you gain a handle on the situation or at least your own decision-making process. There is a reason that elite performers from Michael Jordan to Serena Williams use mindfulness to help.

The message here is: know your biology. When faced with a decision, first check in with how you're feeling in yourself. Can you take a moment to just breathe? If you've got a bit more time, think about how healthy you've been over the last week. Have you been sleeping well? Eating regular meals? Avoiding excessive amounts of alcohol? Or are you on the back of a several-day fast-food binge, washed down with cans of local IPA – and did you spend last night staring into the empty abyss that is social media on your phone until you eventually fell asleep at 4am? If the answer is yes, you're probably not mentally ready to juggle a life-changing least-worst decision. If you absolutely have to go ahead with it, you'll very likely find yourself falling into the inertia traps we identified in the last chapter.

Who Am I?

The study of decision-making is, in part, woven around an understanding of different personality types and individual differences: because, just as personality affects, for example, how strongly an individual interacts with others (extrovert), how self-contained they are (introvert), how antisocial (sociopath), how diligent (conscientious), and so on, it also affects an individual's potential to make decisions efficiently, especially those decisions we have already identified as the hardest decisions of all to make – least-worst decisions.

For the past few years, with partners in the United States and United Kingdom Armed Forces, we have been on a journey to discover the ingredients of the 'perfect' least-worst decision maker. The reason is simple: we want to make sure that the people that they are hiring, training and promoting are the right people to make hard choices. In order to answer this question, we developed an inventory of least-worst decisions, which we refer to as 'LUCIFER' (the Least-Worst Uncertain Choice Inventory for Emergency Responses). In LUCIFER training, participants face a range of situations in which they have to juggle equally uncertain and unappealing decisions, and must commit to a course of action. These decisions involve a range of contexts and put the decision maker in a multitude of new and uncertain situations.

For example, we present the decision maker with the following situation:

> Hi, we have a bit of a situation. I am downtown and there is a kid on top of a building. It's about 15 floors high. He has been up there for a few hours, but now he is threatening to jump if we don't move our perimeter further up the street. I don't want to aggravate him, but moving the perimeter could threaten public safety. What do you want me to do?

After they have made their decision, we then give them another 'inject'. In this case: 'Captain, he is now demanding that we bring him a pizza. What should we do?'

The scenario is designed to be ambiguous; it is designed not to give the person all the information that they need. We want to challenge our participants and we like it when they disagree with each other. We are not so much interested in whether they decide to give the kid the pizza or not. We are interested in how hard they find it to make that decision, how long it takes them and what factors about them as a person predict how well they make that decision.

Other scenarios include some we've faced ourselves. Consider, for example, the following from a student trip I (Neil) once led to Portugal:

> You are the professor on a study abroad trip to Portugal. Last night one of the students had too much to drink and his advances had been rejected by one of the other students. At the end of the night, he found himself on the rooftop deck of the accommodation and knocked a bottle of wine down several storeys and onto the floor below. Luckily it didn't hit anyone, but this could have been a very serious incident. You have since found out that the student has depression and has been having a lot of other issues at home. Protocol says you should send him home but doing so could have negative effects for him in the long run if he is expelled from the trip and fails the course.

What we find in participants' answers is that there is just enough uncertainty for people to have very different reactions. Some people find it incredibly easy and, with little to no thought, immediately declare 'send the troublemaker home'. Others are equally assertive, but declare the exact opposite: 'he stays – everyone deserves a second chance'. In other cases people find themselves agonising over the choice because there is just too much uncertainty and no real chance of clarity: 'If he stays he could do it again (or worse), but if I send him home am I overreacting and potentially ruining his future over nothing?'

And this is precisely our design. Because in all cases like these, there is no 'right' answer, and indeed there is no way for the decision maker to know what is 'right'. They may have immensely different interpretations of what will/ would happen if they choose either option, and the truth is that (like in many real-world decisions) they will not know precisely what will happen. But again, we are not measuring if they do the right thing, we are interested in who is better able to overcome uncertainty and commit to a decision in general. We also measure how *hard* they find the decisions as well as if they embrace the higher-risk options that have the greater potential for *good*, or the more avoidant choices that minimise the chances of further harm.

Over the past three years, we have run thousands of people through the LUCIFER scenario. Perhaps our most impressive achievement was working with the Army Research Institute's Foundational Science Research Unit to collect data from over 250 soldiers from a range of army bases across the United States. While this was a long research process that involved us living on military bases and running trials on soldiers from 5am, it may have given us the clearest picture yet of how the key personality factors play a role in how well people make least-worst decisions.

The most interesting thing we found may surprise you. It's that the most powerful personality variable we've found useful has nothing to do with a military mindset or handling a situation with high stakes. Instead, it links to how hard we all find it to choose a movie, whether to switch radio station and whether or not to throw away food in the fridge that's a day past its sell-by date.

Maximisers versus satisficers

The questions above all relate to the tendency to try to *maximise* the outcomes of a given situation. Consider this example from virtually every time my wife and I (Neil) go shopping together. As we pull into the car park my wife sees a space, usually nice and open, with no car nearby. 'Oh there is a nice space – why don't you pull in there?' she asks. I usually ignore her, convinced that just up ahead there will be a nice open parking space right by the door to the store. A few seconds extra driving, for a much shorter walk. Alas, as we get up to the door I find that the space I thought was empty actually has a small car already parked there. I internally swear at the owner of the small car, while also trying not to swear as my wife says 'told you so'. I turn back around and hope that the previous car parking space is still there. Usually, it isn't.

We make these kinds of decisions all the time, trying to squeeze the absolute best out of a situation, only to find that our attempt to make everything as good as possible contra-logically made the outcome much worse.

Let's imagine a more serious situation. You live overseas and are returning home for a few days. You're keen to try your absolute hardest to see all the friends and family you have not seen over the past few years. Each of them has asked when you will be home, and you have promised each you will see them when you're back. You land on home shores and spend the next seven days frantically driving, walking, bussing and training all across the country to try to make sure you see absolutely everybody. When you get back on the plane, you realise you're tired, annoyed and disappointed that you did not spend enough time with those who truly mattered, and in all honesty probably annoyed a lot of people by only being able to see them for a brief few hours (or even less).

These situations represent something that the philosopher Alan Watts referred to as a 'backwards law', meaning that the quest for one thing can create the opposite outcome. His view being that, 'The desire for more positive experience is itself a negative experience. And, paradoxically, the acceptance of one's negative experience is itself a positive experience.'[7]

To rephrase via popular blogger Mark Manson, the quest for a positive outcome creates a negative outcome, while the acceptance of a negative outcome creates a positive outcome.[8] Accepting that you can't always get that perfect car parking spot will prevent you from wasting time driving past perfectly open spaces. Accepting that you can't see (and indeed please) everyone when you visit home will ensure that you actually spend the most time with those who are the most important to you. Often, the quest for perfect happiness is the source of our greatest unhappiness.

How we as individuals handle this conundrum is reflected in a personality trait we call 'maximisation'. The distinction between 'maximising' and 'satisficing' was first made by the psychologist Herbert A. Simon in 1956.[9] Simon noted that although fields like economics posited maximisation or 'optimising' as the rational method of making decisions, humans often lack the cognitive resources or the environmental affordances to maximise. Maximisers are therefore those who seek to constantly make the best of a choice, while satisficers (the opposite of maximisers) are better able to settle for an option that is 'good enough'. Surprisingly then, what we've discovered in our work with soldiers and police officers – and we believe this also applies in the rest of life – is that the best decision makers are not people who strive for *perfection*; they're people prepared to settle for *good enough*. Specifically, they know that all things will work out in the end and that, from time to time, sacrifices must be made in order to keep moving forward. That's because, in real-life situations, continuing to hold out for a 'perfect' solution will mean the decision maker runs out of time, and so isn't able to make a decision at all. In other words, the decision maker who waits for everything to be ideal ends up giving away their right to make a choice at all, because time makes the decision instead: the job opportunity isn't there any longer, you lose out on the chance to buy that farm in rural France or you become too old to leave your marriage.

Let us imagine a thought experiment to put this in perspective. I want you to imagine you have gone into an ice cream shop and are just going to observe the people at the counter for ten minutes. In this ten-minute window you will likely see several different 'types' of decision maker. You will see people who go to the counter and buy the same thing every time. You will likely also see people who go to the counter, see something on the menu that seems nice and buy it. And you will likely see a handful of people who spend the entire time in the line discussing their choice – 'I *know* I like chocolate chip, but I think I might just want to try something different, but what if I don't like it?' They may spend the entire time not deciding and delay even further when the cashier asks them what they want: panic, pause and then choose. You may then also watch as, after getting their ice cream and taking their first bite, they utter the words 'I wish I had chosen the chocolate chip.' You have just seen maximisation in action; for better and for worse.

Now take a moment, when you choose ice cream, which pattern best predicts how you choose? This is not to say that we can predict your entire personality based solely on this single decision (for example, I (Neil) am absolutely not a maximiser, but I often panic in ice cream shops and once walked out with an experimental goat's cheese ice cream, which was just awful), but on average, across all decisions, the more often someone finds themselves trying to maximise the more likely it is that they are a trait maximiser.

Maximisers want things to be ideal, but the truth is that life never really is ideal, so they end up making things harder for themselves – not only in terms of decision-making, but in a whole raft of ways. Research shows, for example, that maximisers are more likely to have low self-esteem (they never can be good enough); they have lower levels of happiness (because they're never going to achieve the perfect situation in which they'll be 'truly' happy); and they're likely to be less satisfied than others with how things are going (because somewhere inside, they're waiting for that 'ideal' moment that's never going to come).[10] Maximisers are also more prone to regret, less optimistic, greedier and more neurotic than people who have lower expectations. They're also less open, less happy, have lower overall life satisfaction and lean towards procrastination, which, as we have already seen, can be a hurdle to good decision-making. Our research has found that, in military settings, maximisers are less effective decision makers: they find it harder to make a choice, and they tend to take longer – and taking a long time in a military setting can often mean failure.[11]

In contrast, being someone who can settle with *less* can actually give you *more*. These people are known as satisficers: they know perfection doesn't exist and, instead of seeking it out, they seek out the best realistic option available to them, when presented with a choice.

So, how do you know if you are a maximiser? Well, ask yourself a few questions; how often do you read the whole menu when you go to dinner and struggle to decide what to eat? How often do you spend time fantasising about a life that is 'better' than yours? How often do you think about changing jobs, even if you are perfectly happy at your current one? Better yet, how many hours do you spend surfing Netflix before you are able to pick a movie or show to watch?

If you found yourself agreeing with most of these questions, you are showing traits of a maximiser. This is not necessarily a bad thing, and we absolutely are not advocating that you should never seek to maximise your outcomes. What is important is knowing when you have the opportunity to maximise and when you do not. And in those instances when you do not have the luxury to maximise, be self-aware of your tendencies and override them. Take, for example, moving to a new house. Such a monumental and expensive decision should not be taken lightly, nor should it be rushed. However, if you are moving cities for a new job with your partner and children and you have a starting date of 1 September, 15 August is a bad time to be waiting for a house that has just the right amount of natural light flooding the open-plan kitchen you are looking for. Maximising your outcomes is not a bad thing, but trying to maximise situations when either you do not have the time to do that *or* if you are in a situation in which you cannot realistically have a 'best' outcome, the very attempt to achieve perfection will lead to more pain and anguish. Sometimes we have to know when we can and cannot settle, and, more importantly, we need to know when *we are succumbing to our own personal desire* to maximise, in a situation where it will not help. The same way we use these maximisation scales on soldiers about to deploy to war, it is useful for you to think about this yourself before you plan on tackling a drastic decision. For example, trying to break up with someone in a 'perfect' way in which no one gets hurt is not possible, and often your attempts to avoid anyone experiencing any harm will cause more hurt and confusion.

So: know yourself. What are your own personal tendencies when it comes to making decisions? Do you often try to make the best of a situation? Do you try to please everyone except yourself? What you naturally do will often become even more pronounced under stress and strain, so being aware of your characteristics allows you to stop negative traits from getting in the way when it comes time to make a decision.

Once you know yourself, ask yourself: what are the common errors that I fall foul of? Do I struggle to settle? Do I get lost in the details trying to split hairs about which choice is best? And then, when you face a decision, ask yourself: can I maximise? If not, at what point do I need to stop seeking the absolute best and settle for good enough?

What Is Important to Me?

As I (Neil) wrote the final chapters of my PhD on decision-making I decided to take a break and stumbled upon Mark Manson's *The Subtle Art of Not Giving a F*ck*.[12] In the very first chapter I discovered Manson and I were speaking the same language; he focused on how to overcome doubt and fear, and my focus was on how soldiers handled complex situations at war. In his opening paragraph he wrote that 'the art of not giving a f*ck' did not mean being indifferent, (i.e. caring about nothing; that is psychopathic), but caring about something bigger than what was in front of us – in other words, elevating something else so it was more important than adversity.

This view was the slightly more succinct, and indeed direct, expression of a theory we had developed about how soldiers were able to make some of the hardest decisions imaginable, to live by them, and even thrive in spite of them. Our theory was focused on what we call 'sacred values'; things you care about *so much* that you are willing to suffer adversity and even losses of other things that matter to you. I once interviewed a soldier, who told me about how, on a hilltop in Afghanistan after a 24-hour firefight with the Taliban, he was ordered by a senior officer to launch a search to go into the mountains and get a body count – meaning that the officer wanted the soldiers to travel out into the mountains, in the dark, to calculate how many enemies they had killed so that they could report those numbers back to headquarters. The soldier told me how, in a matter of seconds, he weighed up the safety of his men and his 20-year military career, and told the officer he refused and was taking his team back to base. In his words:

> Talk about paralysis by analysis, there was no paralysis here. For a split second I thought 'this is it, this is my military career' . . . and I said, 'Well, Sir, here's what's gonna happen; the people that are wearing this patch [pointing at his own arm] are gonna get in their vehicles and we're gonna get out of here because this is not a safe place to be. And the people wearing that patch [pointing at the senior officer's arm] can stay here and follow you into the mountains.'

At that point the senior officer got right in his face and was irate, swearing and threatening, telling him that he was disobeying a direct order and he would bring him up on charges. Our interviewee just looked at him and said, 'Well, you do what you have to do Sir and I'll do what I have to do.' And he looked over to his platoon and said 'mount up – let's get out of here' and everybody got in their vehicles (including some of the senior officer's forces) and 'rolled away'.

The soldier did not lose his job, and he continues to have an illustrious career in the United States Army. His assumption is that after the fact, the senior officer realised the futility of his order and did not report the act of disobedience. But in that moment, he was totally and utterly committed to his choice in full knowledge that doing so could result in dishonourable discharge. Can you imagine caring about something so deeply that you could not care less about the consequences? It is almost enviable to think that someone can be so committed to their values, because having a strong sense of what absolutely matters to you is liberating when it comes to making least-worst decisions. Those values and your certainty about them guide what you are able to do and, indeed, what you are not able to do.

The truth is that we all hold values, but often we don't work out which values matter the most. It's not enough to have worked out simply what matters to us; we also need to have derived a hierarchy of which values matter most.

When offered a job in a faraway land, some of us are able to leave our family, pack up a suitcase and chase adventure. For that person, self-achievement is higher in their value hierarchy than staying close to family. For others, remaining close to family will always trump the value of adventure and being far away from home. They may visit foreign lands, but where their family are will always be home.

The most important way we can prime ourselves for effective and speedy decision-making, even around the hardest sorts of decisions, is to take time beforehand to focus on what we care about, and to be aware of what we believe is most important of all in our lives. This is work we can and should do well ahead of needing to make life's big decisions; and, of course, it is helpful in all sorts of ways in our lives. Having a 'hierarchy of values' and understanding what we believe to be most crucial and what our 'sacred values' are helps us become more effective and efficient communicators and individuals because we can assess a situation more clearly from the start, and we're primed to know quickly and easily what route is going to be best for us.

When facing decisions it is often easy to get overwhelmed by all of the factors that are important. Let's take an example in which you have a young child. Let's call the child Luke – he's seven years old. Luke has been at his school for two years and has made several friends. However, one of his best friends left recently and, while he socialises well with his two remaining good friends, he has definitely felt the pain of losing that best friend. Moreover, you notice that the teaching quality has gone down considerably and there seems to be less concern and care for the children generally. Soon, there will be a new school opening up in your near neighbourhood, but that is at least one year away.

Your plan always was to move Luke when that new school opened up. However, you are now contemplating moving him to another school entirely because he is far less happy than he was, you still have another year with him at that school and, of course, he has lost his best friend. If there were other schools in the area, you and your partner would consider them, but there are none. The nearest school is 45 minutes away – at least – and in heavy traffic, considerably more. However, when the three of you visit this school you all agree it's lovely. It's smaller, intimate and you get a really good vibe about the education; the kids there seem very happy. Of course, you have concerns about Luke making new friends as well as leaving friends at his old school, but on the other hand you are worried that another year at his current school could have a detrimental effect. What are you going to decide to do?

In this scenario there are all sorts of issues that you need to think about and organise in order of priority. Maybe you can think of some yourself, but a brief few include:

1. Luke's academic attainment.

2. Luke's happiness.

3. Luke's friends and his ability to still see them.

4. The commute.

5. Moving Luke again in a year.

There's no right or wrong here: for some parents, making sure that Luke does not lose touch with his current friends may be the most important thing, while for others it could be making sure his attainment is not disrupted.

How do you therefore navigate these many competing values and priorities and work out what the right decision *for you* is? Well, you need to identify what the *sacred* value(s) are – that is, those that you would never sacrifice. You may know what these are; you may feel it in your gut. If not, there are a few questions you can ask yourself to help identify what you hold sacred. For example, ask yourself the following: has my opinion on a value or stance changed over time? Has it ever? Would it ever? Or: would I be willing to make a sacrifice against this value, even if it means giving up on something I really want?

If your answer to these questions is 'no', better yet, a 'resounding no', you have identified a sacred value.

Over the past few decades psychologists have shown that sacred values guide all sorts of behaviour that we otherwise fail to explain rationally.[13] When something is sacred to us, we will go to the ends of the earth to protect it, even if we stray so far as to become *irrational*. Protecting the values that are important to you is critical. Imagine for a moment that you take the decision to move Luke to the new school, and after three days he gets in the car, frustrated and angry. He talks about how much he misses his old school and his old friends. He is angry at you for 'forcing' him to leave. Knowing that you made the *right* decision for the *right* reasons will help you make sure that you can handle any temporary bumps in the road – knowing full well that in a few short weeks Luke will be fully integrated, have made new friends and be in a school that is better for him in the long run.

Doing right by yourself is a central pillar in decision-making and psychologists increasingly recognise the immense trauma that can come from actions that are not value-consistent. When we think of the trauma that military personnel and others who work in extreme environments face, we often think of the *physical* trauma that stems from being on the front line. But psychologists are increasingly seeing the effects of the long-term trauma that stems from doing (or even seeing) things that violate our own sacred values. This has been referred to by Brett Litz, a clinical psychologist with the National Center for Post-traumatic Stress Disorder, as 'moral injury' and it involves incidents in which someone perpetrates, fails to prevent, or witnesses an act that transgresses deeply held moral beliefs. It is this experience that then causes long-term, negative emotional, psychological, behavioural, spiritual and social consequences.[14] Moral injury is associated with a range of negative emotional, social and psychological outcomes such as depression, PTSD and alcoholism, and it stems from being unable to overcome the cognitive dissonance that exists between who you believe you are and the decisions or actions that you did, or were party to. Moral injury is a term applied to more than just military figures; we now discuss it as a source of trauma in nurses, doctors and police officers. We will talk about how to build your resilience to this in Chapter 8, but for now, it is just important to know that following your values protects you.

This is why knowing *what you really care about* genuinely does matter. It is not just that it guides action; it also protects you from the natural negative emotions that you will feel regardless of what you do. If you break up with a partner and leave a relationship, knowing that you are doing the right thing is why you are able to recover and eventually move on. If you decide to live 5,000 miles away from your family, remembering you're chasing your professional dream of a lifetime will dent the heartbreak of missing them. If you opt to resign from your company and leave the colleagues you've been through a lot with, believing in your new role at the new organisation will help you cope without them.

Values guide us, but they also protect us. It is when we act, and then realise that we followed the wrong value, or, worse, acted based on values we thought were important to us when in fact they belonged to someone else, that we often will struggle the most with what we have done. This is why it is so important that when you face the hardest decisions in life you do not just ask yourself what matters to you, but truly reflect on what is sacred to you — what value must you absolutely make sure that you protect when making this decision?

Values, and specifically knowing what we have decided we value most of all, lie at the heart of decision-making. Knowing our values is key because, as we have already explained, making a decision is much less about what might happen in the future and far more about taking a step that reflects what we believe to be important right now. Remaining true to ourselves is essential: in fact, there's plenty of research to show that regretting a decision is much more to do with feeling you betrayed your values than it is about how events pan out.[15]

Taboos and Trade-offs

As Amelia found when faced with the decision we described at the start of the chapter about what sort of treatment to have for cancer, choices are driven by values – because values help us decide which trade-offs we are and are not willing to accept as a consequence of our choice. If you already know your values, you will find it much easier – indeed, it can be almost automatic – to know what values are, for you, absolute, i.e. they can't be traded off or against. These inviolable, or sacred, values are infinitely more important than other values, and attempting to trade off against them can lead to negative emotional reactions including blame, guilt and avoidance. 'Lesser' values are known as 'secular' values; they matter, but they're not sacrosanct. Examples of secular values might be:

- never being late
- always keeping up-to-date with filing your paperwork
- stopping work to chat to your kids when they come in from school
- being polite to your neighbours

Making decisions means weighing up different issues you hold dear (your 'values') and deciding which one you're going to jettison in order to keep the other. These are called trade-offs, and they fall into three distinct categories. First up is the 'routine' trade-off, in which two secular values are pitted against one another. Perhaps your children's arrival home coincides with a big deadline for the project you're working on: it's relatively easy to override the value (or in this case, postpone it for later when you've finished what you need to do) because you need to get your work through its crux point.

The second sort of trade-off is what's known as 'taboo', and it happens when a secular value is up against a sacred value. Say that, as you're hurrying along the road to an important appointment, an elderly person falls a few steps ahead of you on the pavement. Your secular value of always being on time is instantly trumped by your sacred value to help someone in need – even though stopping to help is going to make you arrive late.

These two trade-offs are fairly easy to negotiate, but then we come to the trickiest type, which are pretty much in a category of their own. They're known as 'tragic' trade-offs because they involve making a choice between two sacred values, and that makes it very difficult indeed to make the call. Think back to the tunnel scenario we discussed at the start of Chapter 1 (page 9) – the reason it was such an agonising choice was because every option involved a value we'd all identify as sacred, which is our need to preserve human life at all costs. But in that scenario, the cost itself brought the risk of violating the value. In ordinary parlance, tragic trade-offs are what we call impossible situations: whichever way we turn, we run the risk of ending up responsible for an action that contravenes a sacred value. These are the situations where decision-making is hardest, and also where inertia – which we believe is the biggest hurdle we face to being effective decision makers – is most likely to occur, because we are wired to avoid sacrificing what we hold most dear; and in our deepest selves, one of the things we fear most is the loss that comes with realising that we have sacrificed something we hold most dear. So rather than risk feeling that sense of loss, we attempt to hold on to two possibilities, not realising that by doing so we are giving up any possibility of being able to shape events.

Let's look an example that we often use in our trainings from the corporate world. I want you to imagine that you are the CEO of 'Operation Efficacy', a company you started up two years ago and have invested heavily in. Your company produces training programmes and platforms to enhance staff performance. Lloyd Merry is your statistician and he has been with the company since its inception. Lloyd is highly intelligent and performs complex analysis on how effective your innovative programmes are. Lloyd is the hardest-working, most loyal and most liked employee you have. However, in the past Lloyd has had some issues with his personal hygiene and several members of staff have commented on this (in passing and behind his back) after meetings. You are unsure if Lloyd is aware of this, but you have noticed that his confidence when presenting in pitches is getting lower. Over the past year, you have been partnered with Estriver, which is a social media consultancy, and with their help you have grown your profit margin by 235 per cent, allowing you to recruit 15 new members of staff. However, with the recent uncertainty of the financial markets, Estriver is considering breaking off the agreement between the two companies, citing concerns about their own 'return on investment'. Your bosses have made it incredibly clear to you that this is the most important meeting yet and their view of you (positive or negative) will be directly affected by how this goes.

You are set to have a meeting with the senior leadership of Estriver, and Lloyd is a key part of your presentation.

Ten minutes before the meeting is set to begin, a friend of yours who you came up through the company with comes to you. She is a good friend, but is also directly competing with Lloyd for a likely future promotion. She enters your office and says she is 'gravely' concerned about Lloyd. She walked past him earlier and said that his poor hygiene is worse than usual. He looked dishevelled, unkempt and really is quite pungent. You have five minutes to decide what to do.

While this decision may seem quite benign, you would be surprised at how many people struggle with this scenario. This is especially true if we add in information about who Lloyd is. We often give a brief that Lloyd came from a poor working-class family and is one of six children. Lloyd worked hard in school and was the first in his family to go to university, juggling three jobs and studying. His work ethic is outstanding due to his drive to give back to his parents and provide a better life for them, especially since his father was diagnosed with heart disease a year ago. Lloyd also cares for his father when he's got the rare chance off work.

At this point, this decision is getting really tough; on the one hand we have a must-nail presentation that involves our most important partner, with work that you are directly responsible for (and your bosses know it), while on the other is someone who is clearly working incredibly hard, is the only person who knows the numbers well enough to present them and potentially has put aside various possibly personal matters and stresses to make sure that he is ready to give the presentation. Thinking about our values, we have a toxic mix of wanting to do what is best for us, the company, our future and our family, and being a good friend, a good colleague, and a good person and protecting Lloyd.

In this scenario, we know what we want, but it is deciding what we are willing to sacrifice that makes it so difficult. Could you walk into that meeting knowing that you had just had to tell Lloyd he cannot join? Or could you allow Lloyd in, knowing that protecting him and his career is potentially jeopardising your own? It is this juxtaposition of values that makes this decision so difficult. When it comes to toxic trade-offs, you have to make sure you know what you are actually trading off against. This is not easy in the moment, but as we highlighted above, sometimes you need to take a breath, calm down and get over the immediate stress and focus on what is really at play in this decision. In many cases, decisions involve values that reflect on who we are as a person, and that is not something that should be traded away lightly.

Now you know more about trade-offs and how they affect decision-making, think about how they've played out in your own life. You've probably automatically made choices around taboo or lesser trade-offs, but knowing that's what you're doing may help you be quicker and more decisive in knowing what to do in some situations. And when it comes to tragic trade-offs, it's important not only to recognise what's taken place, but also what the fallout will be in your own life. Coming up against a tragic trade-off will always leave you with heartache and difficult emotions to work through: be kind to yourself, and give yourself time to deal with these.

DECISION TIME TIPS

1. Do not neglect your biology – if you don't look after the basics (diet, exercise and sleep), you are compromising your ability to decide. It doesn't matter how you take care of these, but you must give them some attention since your brain resides in your body and is subject to biological effects.

2. Think about the things that make you 'you'. These include individual differences, personality and your values and belief systems. In order to optimise how you make decisions, an honest appraisal of what you value and how you think is necessary. You can't prioritise a key goal unless you can clearly articulate what you care most about and what you value. In particular, we'd recommend getting a sense of whether you are a maximiser or satisficer. Knowing you're the former makes you aware that you're vulnerable to delay, and if you're the latter it will help you to know you have a tendency to being impulsive.

3. Know when your tendencies are an asset, and a hindrance. There is nothing wrong with being a maximiser! But when you have a three-minute window to do the shopping it's not the time to try to get the best parking space possible. By knowing what your personality traits are, you can identify when they are a help, or a hindrance.

4. Articulate your key values since these will always influence how you prioritise one decision (a sacred value) over another (a secular one). When faced with a critical decision, always write down the things you value about the decision. Look at your list and decide which issues are negotiable and which are not. The latter are your sacred values, and if they collide against one another, you will need to tease them apart to avoid the paralysing impact of decision inertia.

CHAPTER 4

Stories and Situations

T HE FIRST THING Webb noticed was the shirt.

White. Pristine.

'Too white. Too pristine,' said a voice at the back of his mind.

He'd been at dinner the previous evening when a number he didn't recognise flashed up on his mobile phone. He picked up, and a man's voice said he had intelligence he wanted to give the Americans.

Webb was a US army major, on a tour of Afghanistan. The man on his phone was someone known to the military as a 'walk-in': a member of the public who voluntarily offers information. Webb talked to him for a few minutes and said he'd call him back: the procedure with walk-ins was to get them into the base to conduct an interrogation.

He and his colleagues hatched a plan for the pick-up: the informant was asked to be on a particular street at a specific time, to give a prearranged signal when he saw Webb and then to raise his hands so he could be searched before being put into a vehicle and taken to the base for an interview. As soon as the informant appeared it was clear to Webb that this was their man, but he didn't give the signal they'd agreed, he just walked right over to them – and a split second after realising that, Webb also saw something that gave him pause; the man's shirt was too white. 'Everyone in Afghanistan wears white clothes, but they're never actually white,' Webb explained to us. 'Because of the dust and the heat the white was always dirty. But this guy: he was wearing pristine, clean white.'

Alarm bells now ringing, Webb ordered the soldiers to force the walk-in to the ground and search him properly, but as they did, something else started to happen. The lights on an SUV parked across the street suddenly came on and the car started to move towards them.

When he thought about it afterwards, Webb realised he'd already clocked the SUV. 'It looked like a very nice car for that area – and also, it had tinted windows, which are unusual in Afghanistan.'

By now, Webb had realised there was a chance he and his men were under attack, and that the SUV was going to run them over or – even worse – might be packed with explosives. In a split second, he had to decide: should he shoot at the oncoming car and risk killing an innocent civilian behind the wheel or not act, leaving the lives of everyone in his team, and passers-by in the immediate vicinity, at risk?

Webb's dilemma is the sort of life-and-death decision that soldiers face on a fairly regular basis, and though most of us are not members of the military, and never will be, we can all learn from the way they make their choices.

What is critical to understand is that what Webb does, and indeed what he believes is right, is based on his interpretation of what is going on; how he threads a narrative that links all of these disparate events together (the phone call, the walk-in, the SUV and now) to create his understanding of what is going on.

Captain Webb was a real-life soldier interviewed by us as part of our research into how soldiers make decisions under pressure: the incident we are describing really took place, and indeed was the hardest decision Webb says he faced during his many deployments. He was very aware of what was at stake in this situation, and while he knew he was legally within the rules of war to shoot, in his words:

> But there is the other side of me that looks at it and says, you know, that if I fired and wasn't supposed to, not only would that have probably ended my career, forget my career, I would have had to have lived the rest of my life knowing I had killed that guy. I don't know what other people's impression of the military is, if we take these decisions lightly, but I certainly didn't and I don't think other soldiers do either. And the idea that you become jaded to the point when you stop caring about hurting innocent people, I can't imagine becoming that jaded about that decision. In fact, it still bothers me to this day, the idea that I, in a fraction of a second, could have shot that guy, and if he was

Taliban, great. But if he wasn't, I can't imagine the thoughts that would go through my head about that guy's family, and things like that. So, it is a hard decision to live with.

Storytelling

Humans are storytellers: internally, as much as externally. As we navigate the world around us we constantly find ourselves telling and creating stories about what's going on. When someone is rude to a clerk in a store, we tell ourselves a story about who that person is, why they are the way they are – and even a future story in which they get their comeuppance for how they just behaved. We tell ourselves stories about who we are and our place in the world.

Stories are important to us because they help us make sense of the uncertainty of being human. We create stories to fill in the blanks about what we do not know. Stories are our way of making sense of what is going on around us, and that's why they're the first stage of our 'STAR' model of decision-making – because they're where decisions begin. The need to 'make sense' of our surroundings is so central to being human that psychologists Chater and Loewenstein have highlighted the existence of a "drive for sense-making" which comparable to other drives such as hunger, thirst and sex.[1] This innate drive, just like all our other drives, is constantly underpinning our behaviour, pulling us towards things that help us make sense of a situation

Have you ever played Cluedo? In this game you work to unpack a series of clues to allow you to narrow down the murderer, the murder weapon and the room where it happened. You start off with little to no knowledge, just a very few pieces of information, and you work to reveal as much information as possible. At some point, you think you know what is going on. Your heart starts to race and you get increasingly convinced that you know exactly what cards are in the centre. You make your prediction, with utmost confidence, and, just then, as the cards are revealed with a flourish and you expect your moment of triumph, you are told that you are wrong. And indeed, you've now lost the game.

This is the reverse end of our need to know what is happening. We can also often be fooled by being led down garden paths before being presented with the 'real' story. Modern media often plays on our need to create stories in order to surprise, shock and amaze us. How many times has a movie led you to believe you know what is going on, only to be shocked when the true story is revealed? Had you really solved Christian Bale's trick in *The Prestige* before the great reveal (we won't spoil it)? Did you see the twist coming in *Us* before it was revealed to you?

In a board game evening with friends, beyond some bruised pride, no harm comes from leaping to conclusions. At the movies, the more invested we are in the *wrong* story, the better the reveal. We mark a good movie with quotes such as 'I *never* saw that coming' and immediately rewatch it to see the clues we missed and the signs that we missed or ignored before. We know, though, we'll never get that same thrill of being tricked as we did the first time we saw it.

Real life, though, is different: here, the stories we make have much more far-reaching consequences, and we cannot simply rewatch to see what we missed the first time around. We do not get to make a guess, find out we were wrong and then re-evaluate and have another go. So *how* we develop our story of the world, and what conclusions we draw from it, are vital. For Captain Webb, as for all of us, how we interpret the few clues we have in a momentous situation, and how we act based upon that, could live with us forever.

The aim of this chapter is to show you the psychological process of storytelling and the important role it plays in decision-making. We want you to be able to understand how this process works, and often how it perhaps falls apart, so that you can start making decisions with the right footing. What novices often do wrong is misunderstand the situation early and commit to (or even double down on) their incorrect assessment. Experts, on the other hand, are more open-minded – they are receptive to the idea that there are several possible explanations for what they are seeing – and rather than overcommitting to an action based on a single diagnosis, they take time to make sure they know precisely what is going on.

By the end of this chapter we want you to be able to think like expert storytellers, which means holding judgement until you are sure and working hard to imagine all possible outcomes, rather than just the first (or even most likely) one that comes to mind.

Situational Awareness

'Situational awareness' is an important element of decision-making. In plain English, what that means is 'you need to work out what's going on'. This is the preliminary stage of any decision you'll ever take, and it covers three distinct stages that throw events forward as well as assessing what's already taken place. This is what's involved:

1. Understanding what has already happened.

2. Understanding why it is happening.

3. Predicting from this what is going to happen next.

Now, if that sounds easy, it's definitely not – not in military situations, especially, where elements of what's happening are often unknown, and not in civilian life either. Say your partner comes home one day and is surprisingly quiet; you do not hear from a close friend for a few weeks at a time; your boss has failed to email about that promotion they said was in the pipeline. In all these cases, there is no 'easy' or 'certain' story here, but how we handle this process of trying to develop the story plays an important role in our decision-making process. Can you hold off judgement and explore what might be going on or do you immediately jump to the worst-case scenario (in this case, 'they all hate me')?

For most decisions, most of the time, there isn't a full picture. You have to be on the lookout for clues and you have to build on experience and instinct – and, if time is short, you have to be ready to take a decision without having fully answered all the questions you want to ask, simply because time is running out. That's the bit many people find hardest to compute – they think that because they don't know enough, they can't make a decision. But what we say is: do nothing and the decision will make itself for you. Making good decisions means honing certain skills, and one of these is being sharp and on-message about what's going on around you.

Let's go back to Captain Webb. In stage one of situational awareness, he needed to identify what was happening, and that meant being on the lookout for clues about what was, or might be, going on. He clocked straight away that the informant on the street looked odd – with unusually clean clothes – and that was unusual. Then came the SUV. While he didn't know exactly what was going on, he did know instinctively that something didn't seem right. To make matters worse, Webb had recently spoken to some friends who were hit with a vehicle carrying an improvised explosive device and the one thing they said about the incident was that 'things looked out of place'.

In stage two, Webb attempted to piece together what he was experiencing: an informant who seemed to be behaving oddly and who was wearing clothes that seemed suspicious; a car that was behaving erratically, that pulled out of its parking space at the precise moment that the informant was wrestled to the ground. What was going on here? Webb is a soldier, he's operating in a war zone, so he's primed for recognising the signs that he might be under attack. As he himself said, the pointers in this case were that things were not as he would have expected them to be.

Stage three is the most critical of all in decision-making, because it goes to the heart of what it's all about. It's the sixty-four-thousand-dollar question: what is going to happen next? And in this case, Webb's mind was predicting that what *might* be about to happen was an attack – a very serious, deadly attack in which soldiers and others in the vicinity, including the man now on the ground, might be killed or injured.

In the end, Webb did not shoot, and he was correct because the driver of the SUV was actually a disgruntled neighbour of the man he was trying to meet. The neighbour was trying to scare the man, not knowing that the tactic he chose was the same as an insurgent looking to kill. But Captain Webb did not know this, and he had to use the few cues that he had to quickly decide on a story and make a decision.

As Webb went through the three stages of situational awareness, there is a lesson here that speaks to how each one of us assesses what is going on, and specifically when we think something is going wrong. In military terms, what Webb is talking about is often called 'pattern of life'. It is the instinct we have for what *should* be happening in a certain place, at a certain time. It's an incredibly powerful aid to decision-making because by knowing *what should happen*, we are often able to detect when something is going on that shouldn't be. Even when we do not know what is going on, knowing that *something is wrong* can be crucial because it can begin the search for information – it's an early alert system, if you like. From the studies we did with soldiers when I (Neil) worked at Porton Down, we found (unsurprisingly) that pattern of life tended to develop over the course of a deployment, and that it developed more quickly the longer someone had been on deployment.[2]

You can use the idea of pattern of life to help when you assess a situation and to identify when something might be wrong. Think about when we go to work at 9am, for example. You expect there to be a lot of people – on the roads, on the train, at the office and on your way home. When you go home, you expect the same. But if you go home particularly late one evening, you expect this traffic to be lighter. In life you have expectations of what should be happening. Deviations in this are then markers that something is different or unexpected. Imagine walking into your office at 9am and it is completely empty. You would ask yourself: what is going on? Is there a company training event I forgot about? Is today a national holiday I missed? In the same vein, if you get on the train after a long day at 9pm and find it is packed full you may wonder if there is a concert, gig or even protest going on that has caused this mass of people.

In your interpersonal relationships, when you come home to your family or meet an old friend, you have expectations of how you will be greeted and how you will react. Sometimes you may notice someone is slightly *off* with you. A friend is not as warm as they usually are; your partner does not immediately acknowledge your return home. In these instances, you have probably felt that deviation: 'Something just doesn't feel right.' The mistake in these instances is to immediately create a story to fill in the blanks and explain why that person did not behave in the way you expected; to decide what the story is, and to then act as though it is real. We call this a form of bad thinking, and the deeply human tendency to focus on a single possible story – the 'runaway train' – and we cover this in detail in Chapter 6 (see page 143).

What happens when situational awareness goes awry?

Being 'primed' to expect things to go a certain way is a central element of decision-making, and it's worth unpacking why. Psychologists have long known the extraordinary power of confirmation bias: what that means is that the human brain, once it's hit on a particular explanation for something, is wired to seek out evidence that supports it. In 2011, psychologists Hugo Mercier and Dan Sperber took this idea a stage further and suggested that reasoning was a mechanism designed by evolution not for arriving at the truth, as we might have liked to think, but instead to systematically find arguments that justify one's beliefs or actions.[3] It is easier to be told that we are right than to have to engage in the cognitive process of deciding if we are right to begin with. Furthermore, when looking for confirmation, we often don't look for an exact source of confirmation, but instead settle for any evidence that confirms our interpretation; when trying to work out what is going on, we do not look at what is around us and evaluate it all, but instead look for one thing that agrees with what we think is going on and use that to support our assessment.

This psychological process is immensely powerful; it's the bedrock of social media and all that's wrong with it, and the overwhelming success of that phenomenon would seem to point to Mercier and Sperber's theory being correct. Once we've got an idea in our heads, we're hungry for confirmation that we're on to something. In other words, we are designed not to be objective, and that goes against us in terms of the efficacy of our decision-making. We attend to information that agrees with what we already think, we search out information that tells us things we already believe about the world and we often avoid sources of information (including people) who will tell us things that do not align with our world view. Overall, when people study errors in major decisions, most often they stem from an inability to understand what is going on in front of them.

Situational awareness is fundamental to military operations, as we've already seen; but it's equally important in the big decisions of our personal lives. Eight years ago, Jenny, then aged 40, discovered her husband of 11 years, Rob, was having an affair with a colleague at work. Yes, she'd had some suspicions – he seemed more evasive these days and he made several complimentary comments about the new colleague that seemed more than just how professional and helpful she was. But, still, finding out what in the back of her mind she had considered felt like an enormous blow. She hadn't fully suspected that Rob was having another relationship and she hadn't been looking for evidence of it: she found the messages from his colleague, Cindy, telling Rob she loved him, on his mobile phone while innocently searching for something else.

The discovery stopped Jenny in her tracks: suddenly she was in entirely uncharted territory. Clearly there were decisions to make about her relationship with Rob, but first, she had to work out what was going on, why it was happening and what was likely to happen next.

The presenting issue was very clear, and for Jenny it was stage one awareness of what was happening. Rob and Cindy were having an affair. But what Jenny needed to find out was whether they loved one another; if they did, that might be a game changer for her marriage. Jenny and Rob's three children were at the time aged ten, seven and three. Jenny believed strongly in family life; she knew Rob was a good father to their children, and she didn't want her children to grow up with divorced parents unless there was absolutely no alternative.

Beyond finding out whether Rob loved Cindy (and even whether Cindy really did love Rob), Jenny knew she had to think about why the affair was going on. She was very aware that she and Rob had grown apart since the arrival of the children; they both had busy jobs and there seemed to be less and less time for one another – in fact, both of them had failed to prioritise their relationship for some years. So her stage two awareness that the affair was happening was at least partly to do with pressures on the marriage, but perhaps not with fundamental problems in the marriage itself.

As to stage three, Jenny was pretty sure, when she thought about what was likely to happen next, that Rob and Cindy probably didn't want to leave their marriages and set up home together. Cindy was married and the mother of two young children; and there was no way, Jenny knew, that Rob would want to opt out of a domestic life with his own three children to spend it instead with someone else's kids. In short, Jenny realised that, while her husband's affair was a shattering event in her life, the circumstances in which she found herself didn't add up to an inevitable end to her marriage. Instead, she and Rob decided to have relationship counselling. Rob eventually ended his relationship with Cindy, and eight years on Rob and Jenny are happier than they've ever been.

In this instance, we can very realistically think about an alternate reality in which Jenny learned of the affair and immediately came to the conclusion that Rob and Cindy were in love, and the marriage was over. She could have then proceeded to find any and all evidence to support this strongly held view, and from there it is likely that their marriage would have been irreparable. Similar to the game of Cluedo, once you have made your guess, you do not often get a second chance.

This is not to take what Jenny did lightly, because in many cases after learning that something is wrong, especially when it comes to a loved one, our minds work overtime to develop a fully fledged narrative to fill in the gaps, which, though it makes complete sense at the time, often in hindsight seems rather far-fetched.

We saw in the last chapter how our physical and cognitive state can play into how we choose. We should not decide to take a course of action when we know we aren't in the best place mentally or physically. The hardest situations to work out are the ones in which we are stressed, short of sleep, not eating properly and run down. To be properly aware of the situation around us, we must first make space – both physically and mentally – to be the best versions of ourselves possible in the circumstances. Only then can we work out what is going on, why it's going on and what's likely to happen next. And if we can do those things, we're well on the road to making a decision we won't regret. Sometimes, and if we are in a fast-moving environment (like Webb was), we have little say in when we start formulating our situational model. But, in Jenny's case, she was right not to come to any firm conclusions in the immediate aftermath of finding out about the affair. Tempting though this may be, instead she sought to find the space and time to develop her thoughts on what had happened, why it had happened and what might happen next.

Imagine your brain is a pint glass and it is already full of water due to the cognitive load induced by stress. In trying to formulate your situational awareness you are trying to pour more water in an already full glass. So, you need to 'tip some out' and create space in the glass. To do this we need to buy some time. It may sound trite, but simply removing yourself from the immediate environment, getting fresh air and moving gives you headspace and physical space.

One of the most admirable commanders I (Laurence) knew working in the counterterrorism world would, when right in the thick of the action, simply remove himself from the ops room and walk around the outside of the building. Sometimes this would be a five-minute lap; other times several laps, which could take up to an hour, depending on the urgency and complexity of the incident. This approach gave him the mental space he needed to spend time diagnosing what he was dealing with. Inevitably he would come back calmer and with a clearer idea of what was happening, why it was happening and what could happen next. This calm wave of clarity would wash over the rest of the team and they would then set to work resolving the incident.

Ensuring, within reason, you apportion sufficient time to figuring out what you are dealing with is critical since, if you get that wrong, everything that follows flows from a misdiagnosis. If your doctor is too casual in checking your symptoms and thinks you have wind but in fact you have the early signs of pancreatic cancer you may end up dying as a result. Of course, some things are easier to diagnose than others – pancreatic cancer is, for example, one of the harder tumours to spot. The rarer the event, the less likely we are to recognise it. To take another example: you have a fallout with your boss, which you too quickly put down to her having lost confidence in your skills. But it turns out, some time later, that the reason she was stressed was that her mother was seriously ill in hospital.

Critical incidents are by their very nature rare, as are events such as the one that Jenny faced (at least within one person's lifetime). That is, in part, why we struggle with such events. We have no doctrine to follow or policy book on what to do in a break-up and we have no or probably very little prior experience (at least in terms of a potential dissolution of a marriage). Therefore, Klein's notion of recognition-primed decision-making (RPD, see page 18) brings little comfort, since we have no expertise in dealing with these sorts of events. All this can leave us feeling stranded, alone and unable to know where to start. When a major life event of this sort hits us we need to be in the best possible place to deal with it – psychologically and physically. In our work with military personnel and police, individuals facing traumatic events fare far less well if they have other underlying psychological or physical issues. We address psychological and physical readiness in Chapter 8. By all means, dive into that section now if you want to learn more. You will see how we talk about the four pillars of resilience (page 204) that you need to give some love and attention to all the way through your life in order that you are generally more resilient.

As we have seen, when it comes to facing new situations, it is important that you do not let your first gut judgements get the better of you. Yes, we are all intuitive scientists and yes we are designed to try to make sense of this world. But that does not mean that we get it right first time, every time. The skill is knowing how long you are able to hold off making a commitment to a story and how long you have to make an assessment. Ask yourself how long you have to interpret the situation and invest as much time as you can looking at all of the composite parts. Think to yourself, 'What am I looking at?' And if the scene is abstract, what are the multiple things that it *could be* and how can you confirm which one it is? This is how we navigate situational awareness.

Imagining the Worst

On 7 December 1941, just before 8am, hundreds of Japanese fighter planes descended on the US Naval base at Pearl Harbor, Hawaii. The Japanese fighters managed to destroy or damage eight battleships and over 300 aeroplanes. The attack resulted in the death of more than 2,400 Americans.

On 11 September 2001, four planes were hijacked by terrorist offenders associated with al-Qaeda and flown into strategic targets across the United States. Two planes flew into the World Trade Center in New York City; one plane flew into the Pentagon in Washington DC; and the final plane, United Airlines Flight 93, crashed near Shanksville, Pennsylvania, after the passengers heroically fought against the four hijackers. Flight 93's target is believed to have been the Capitol or the White House.

On 8 December 1941, less than 30 hours after the attack on Pearl Harbor, President Franklin D. Roosevelt declared war on Japan. This war eventually resulted in the use of the atomic bomb on the town of Hiroshima.

On 12 September 2001, then-president George W. Bush declared the war on terror.[4] Twenty years later, we are still at war in Afghanistan, and over 3,500 members of the Armed Forces have died. To date over 310,000 civilians have been killed in the fighting since 2001 (the vast majority killed by insurgent forces).

What both these events have in common is that, in review, many expert commentators – from political analysts on television to psychologists – have explored the situational awareness that people had at the moments leading up to the attacks and how these large-scale attacks were able to occur without being detected. The truth is that, in hindsight, we see that the evidence was there, the situation was just not assessed correctly. Articles such as 'How (almost) everyone failed to prepare for Pearl Harbor' now abound and in the review of the intelligence failures that led to 9/11, it is now often repeated that 'the system was blinking red'.[5]

When many people look back on mistakes they have made in their own life, they later admit they experienced the same – 'The warning signs were there and I just ignored them.' How many times have you watched someone date or marry someone despite there being clear early warning signs that they ignored? How many times have you predicted that a friend will not be happy in their new job, despite their confident assertion that they will be? Often we can see when other people are overriding their own intelligence systems and ignoring the warning signs.

So what do these famous cases of situational awareness error have in common, and what can they teach us about our own lives and decision-making? What they tell us is that the most common problem we see is not that people don't have access to the warning signs or that the information that tells us precisely what is going on is *hidden*; we are simply not integrating it and using that information to develop our understanding. The issue is not seeing, or believing, but imagining what is going on.

In our own work on critical incidents, this is one of the issues that we often see: the failure of imagination when it comes to situational awareness. Several years ago, I

(Laurence) had the considerable honour of seeing a senior police officer speak about his team's response to Lashkar-e-Taiba's terrorist attacks on Mumbai in 2008. It was difficult to watch someone so dignified describe what he saw as his own many failings. But, at the centre of his proposal for remediation, was what he described as a failure of imagination. 'None of us imagined this could ever happen – so we never trained for it. What we need,' he continued, 'are foretellers of doom.' After the events of 9/11, the 9/11 Commission Report highlighted a 'failure of imagination'[6] with recommendations including the intriguing proposition that they must routinize, and even bureaucratize, the exercise of imagination.[7]

Grim storytelling

When it comes to trying to work out what is going on around us, we often fail to imagine what could explain the behaviour we're witnessing. Whether it's the intelligence analysts looking at al-Qaeda communications about targeting America or me or you trying to understand why a loved one is suddenly aloof, too often our first instinct is to fail to engage in imagining what the many possible causes of this situation are, and instead fall hard and fast on the first one that comes to mind.

All of which explains why we now train police, the military and emergency responders to imagine events worse than their own experiences. For example, we'll encourage military and police leaders to think about near catastrophes, and to imagine the actual catastrophes that might have played out. We call this cognitively demanding act 'grim storytelling'. The purpose is to generate worst-case scenarios in order to help practitioners learn how to respond. When cautiously and critically facilitated, learning through grim storytelling helps plan for, adapt to and recover from real traumatic events. It's a powerful learning tool that really helps individuals to prepare for scenarios they'd have been unable to imagine otherwise. Storytelling is, in our experience, underutilised as a formal method of learning, despite its universality and primality throughout history.[8]

Now, of course, we are not proposing that we should all engage in repeated acts of grim imaginings ('What if my partner died?', 'What if a nuclear bomb is detonated?', 'What if I crash the car on the motorway?'). Nor are we suggesting that Jenny should see her husband's infidelity as an apocalyptic event in which everything she has believed was not true and he has been cheating for years. But what we need you to be is a foreteller of complexity – for good and for bad. Imagine the different parts of the situation and the complexity of it; think about the interrelation of activities and how they may relate to one another. Jenny should not immediately foresee the apocalypse, but she should consider the possibility that they have fallen out of love, that they may have to divorce and the impact that would have on her, her husband and the children. Why though? Doesn't this pessimistic outlook cause Jenny great suffering and inner angst that may in fact all be untrue? Indeed, such grim imaginings will cause distress, but if they are true and she simply acts like an ostrich they will be considerably more awful when they come to fruition. And it is not as if she has no reason to suspect this might be a possibility – she did not dream up on the basis of no evidence that there is a problem – merely that, as yet, she doesn't know the size of that problem. Our argument is that it doesn't hurt to imagine and thus plan for the worst. Indeed, in not imagining a really bad outcome there is the potential for you to invite it.

It's important to recognise that in imagining the worst, it does not mean that is the only plausible scenario. At the other end of the spectrum, this may be completely benign or at least less bad than you had anticipated. So long as you recognise that the worst-case scenario is just that – a possibility and not a probability – then you can plan accordingly without catastrophising.

In other words, when you're at a critical crossroads, it helps if you can be prepared for a possible bad outcome or outcomes. These might include whether to bring up a sensitive topic with someone at work; whether to allow a friend to crash at your apartment while they look for accommodation; whether to reach out and ask for help at work with a big project that you feel you are struggling with; whether to share your feelings about something you disagree with in a project meeting, and so on. Again, as we saw in the last chapter, it is about having the bravery to think about the problem – being honest with yourself about what the situation involves and what could be happening. Take charge and do not hide away from a negative outcome. If it is indeed the worst-case scenario, are you better off embracing it and preparing, or even making sure that things happen on your terms? Or are you better off hiding and 'hoping for the best', only to then be subject to the exact same outcome? Be bold and embrace the realities of what is going on. You may be surprised at how much better you are able to handle uncertainty when you are open to the real possibilities of what the situation may hold.

Here is an exercise for you to think about as you digest this chapter. Think about some of the hard choices you've faced in the past. If it helps, write them down. Are they mainly family-related, relationship-related or work-related (or indeed a mix)? It's helpful to know if there is a pattern – that way you can increase your predictions about what sorts of things you'll find challenging in the future, especially in those cases where you've avoided acting. Now, for each of these, think about (or write down) what *could* have happened in that situation and ask yourself, 'If it was the worst-case scenario, would I have been better off recognising it earlier and perhaps planning for it?' In many cases, even if it does not come to pass, we would feel better at least knowing what a possible outcome could be. And again, we are not saying that to think of the worst case is to bring it to life, nor to assume that every situation is the worst case (that is just nihilistic). We are saying that good decision-making takes confidence to face the future – both good and bad – and means embracing and thinking about all the *realistic* possibilities that you could face.

It might be tempting to ignore the scariest future, but that can invite more trauma when a less than ideal outcome does emerge. Of course, what can be seen as negative thinking should not be endemic, but when you're faced with a unique or rare event it helps to imagine the worst and the best.

The thing about considering worst-case scenarios is, firstly, that it gives your decision-making a spectrum and allows you to consider the options within the widest framework of your experience. Secondly, it is a more truthful approach: because the truth about life is, unfortunately, that the worst does sometimes happen. If you can take the worst case into account in your decision-making, you are giving yourself the most honest appraisal possible, ahead of making your choice.

Grim storytelling can prepare us for the worst, even if we decide to continue our lives hoping for the best.

DECISION TIME TIPS

1. Elite decision makers hold two or three possible scenarios in their head to try to make sense of what has happened, why it's happened and what may happen next. Having only one scenario in your head will make you more likely to make a mistake, while trying to think up too many options means you risk never getting to grips with the situation.

2. Our advice is that you work out the worst (plausible) outcome and the best (plausible) outcome, and, if you like, one moderate outcome somewhere in the middle. That will give you more than enough to diagnose what's facing you without overloading you.

It also means you can plan for the worst and hope for the best.

3. Always ask yourself the following: what has happened, why has it happened and what are no more than three plausible outcomes of what is possibly going to happen next? You then need to consider two critical things to progress:

(i) Do I have to decide now?
(ii) If I don't, how much time do I have to firm up which of these scenarios is the most likely?

CHAPTER 5

Time Mastery

E VERYONE KNOWS THE story of Goldilocks. What you won't know is that Goldilocks is one of the common analogies that we use to train expert decision makers *when* to make critical least-worst decisions. When it comes to decision-making, it is not just about the decision that we make, we also need to be constantly aware of the balance of time. Like Goldilocks, there is a decision that is too fast, a decision that is too slow and often a decision that is just right. When you meet someone and get married within six months, many would say that is 'too fast'. It may be. But in some cases, if you do not get married within six months you will never be together because one of the partners is on a visa. In this instance, speed is a necessity. In other cases, imagine a friend of yours has been in a job for eight years without a promotion. Perhaps you may think they have stayed long beyond their limit and need to move on. On the contrary, they knew that there was a significant international merger in the pipeline and they are now the director of the New York branch.

It is this ability – to know precisely when you have waited long enough and when you can wait no longer – that seems to separate the greatest from the 'almost great'. In our work, we call this the 'Goldilocks concept' – you have to wait until it is just right.

Because the idea of time is so critical, but also so rarely discussed, we want you to really think about this idea now. Take a minute to think about the role that *time* has played in some of the decisions you have made in your life. How many times have you made mistakes by acting too soon? Do you have a habit of rushing to judgement, diagnosing a problem with little thought of the alternatives (as outlined in the last chapter) and steamrolling, headstrong, into action? Or do you tend to wait too long? Do you lament waiting to tell someone how you felt about them, only for them to fall in love with someone else? Did you fail to follow up with someone who offered you an opportunity?

Finally, think about some of the best decisions you have ever made and ask yourself whether you would have been as successful if you had acted sooner – or later. While it is easy to know that we married 'the one' several years on, this does not mean they would have reacted favourably to being proposed to after six months. Nor would all partners be happy waiting ten years.

The fact is, the 'success' of any decision is as much about when we act, as how we act. And, crucially, it is critical that we know when we *need* to act. This is one of our large issues with 'laboratory' research – it measures what you decide, but it does not allow enough time to truly focus on the science of when you decide. Time, and getting it right, is the essential second step of our 'STAR' model, and in this chapter we'll explain why it's so important and how you can be more aware of it when facing your own tough times and choices.

The key question to ask when you're facing a major decision is the first question the military, police, business and government leaders we work with have to ask when they're faced with a life-or-death decision in a war zone. 'Do I have to act NOW?' If the answer is yes – and for military leaders, it often is – then you have no choice. But very often, with the big decisions in our personal lives, there is time to gather information, and that time is invaluable.

One of the biggest differences between a novice decision maker and an expert is that the expert knows to begin with this question. The novice either doesn't put the decision they have to make into a time frame at all or puts it into a time frame that reduces the power of the situation (of which more later). Time is one of your strongest allies in the decision-making process, but only if you start by working out how much of it you genuinely have, and only if you continually keep a realistic check on it as you assess the information you need and attempt to find out more.

In this chapter we'll pin down exactly how to achieve the 'right' time window for decision-making, but first, here's a key piece of information. Remember what we said in Chapter 3 about perfection – maximisers and satisficers (see page 70)? Good decision makers are not perfectionists, because they realise from the outset that a) perfection is virtually impossible to achieve and b) chasing perfection actually undermines your chances of making a pretty good decision. Ditching the dream of getting everything right will free you to make the best decision you can – and it all starts here, with a realistic assessment of time.

Information-Gathering: How It's Useful (and When It's Not)

Imagine you are staring at the live feed of a compound in Pakistan. On the one hand, you have been told this is where Osama bin Laden is currently residing – and what you do next could lead to the capture of the world's most-wanted terrorist. On the other hand, if you are wrong, you're opening yourself to the charge that you've launched an illegal raid, for no reason, without authority and created a detrimental international incident. Your best guess as to the likelihood of the outcome is fifty-fifty, and despite all the intelligence assets at your disposal, no one can confirm that the shadowy, mysterious figure in the compound is bin Laden. Now, we know how this story ends. And in hindsight former US president Barack Obama made the right choice to launch the mission. But at the time, success was no guarantee and this was certainly no easy decision.

In his book *The Finish*, Mark Bowden leverages access to key White House, military, intelligence and foreign policy officials – including President Obama himself – to tell the inside story of the decision to launch a SEAL Team Six (an elite team of Navy SEALs used for counterterrorism missions) to Abbottabad, Pakistan, to kill Osama bin Laden.[1]

As he recalls, one of the main issues faced by the president was the immense uncertainty surrounding whether Osama bin Laden was in the compound. When the president asked, at the briefing, how confident his colleagues were that bin Laden was in the compound, the estimates ranged from 10 per cent to 95 per cent certainty. As Bowden recalled, it was the president who eventually silenced the room by pointing out that the certainty level was no greater than fifty-fifty and he couldn't make his decision based on the flip of a coin.

During the final discussion on 28 April 2011, the president was briefed on four possible options:

1. A large bombing targeted at the compound. It has a fifty-fifty chance of also killing Osama bin Laden, but would cause a lot of collateral damage.

2. A smaller airstrike using a small missile sent from a tiny drone. Less collateral damage, but this technology had only ever been used in exercises. It was also still only a fifty-fifty chance that bin Laden was there.

3. A ground raid using special forces. The small team could confirm the presence of bin Laden and minimise collateral damage and loss of life. However, this would mean risking the lives of American soldiers and them possibly being caught in Pakistan and accused of taking part in an illegal mission.

4. Do nothing.

As Bowden describes it, Obama asked each of the participants at this final security meeting which of the four options they would take, and to defend their choice. There was no clear agreement in the room and even the vice president (later president) Joe Biden cautioned against the raid, believing that if any option failed, so too would the president's chance of a second term.[2]

Now, mull this over. You have all the intelligence and technology in the world. It is a manhunt for the number one most wanted terrorist in the world, who has evaded capture for over ten years and is responsible for the deaths of thousands of people. The best you have is a 'fifty-fifty' chance of success and the decision is entirely yours. What would you do? Would you defer to the consensus of others? Would you shoulder the burden? What would you decide? The case is fascinating because, alongside so much technology and intelligence, it all boils down to this: a single least-worst decision in which a president's entire legacy is potentially on the line. Every moment that Obama delayed the decision to gain more intelligence, or certainty, the greater the chances that bin Laden leaves the compound, meaning that Obama is back at square one, and just missed the chance to catch the world's most wanted terrorist.

What Obama demonstrated with the bin Laden decision was the importance of knowing when to wait and when to leap. With mounting pressures on all sides, it was surely tempting to delay the choice – he could have waited for more intelligence or for confirmation of more facts. He could have waited for agreement from his top commanders or even got cold feet when his vice president told him that being wrong would be the end of his presidential career. Had he done any of these things, Osama bin Laden could well still be alive today; we would still be searching for the man responsible for the 9/11 attacks and the murder of nearly 3,000 people. But he did not delay; despite the possible negative consequences, he overcame the doubt and fear, and acted.

Make time work for you

Decisions: they're all about what you end up doing, right? Wrong. Decisions are just as much about *when* you do something as they are about what you actually *do*. That's because making a sound decision involves a complicated interplay of many different aspects of being human, and to make the best of all these, your first task is to work out what time frame you have available.

Act too quickly and you'll fail to use experiences that could be helpful, or you'll neglect the opportunity to tap into the values that are important to you and should, as we've already seen, guide you to the course of action that's right for you. Act too slowly and eventually you'll have negated your opportunity to make a decision at all, because events – rather than your intentions – will shape the course of what happens next. Plus, you'll be missing out on the positives of the choice you're sitting on and leaving yourself in an unfulfilled limbo. Obama could have delayed, and bin Laden could have moved, and we could have spent the next ten years searching for the world's most-wanted terrorist.

In a nutshell, the issue around time comes down to this: whatever decision you're facing, if you have time on your side to help you decide, then use it. Let's say you're weighing up whether you want to leave your partner of 20 years or stay with them. On one view of this, time is on your side. Nothing will happen until you make your choice, and it's a life-changing one. Could you be happier alone, or with someone else, than you are with your partner? Might things in your relationship improve and, if so, what do you need to do to ensure they do? If you decide to leave, who else will be impacted by your choice – certainly your children, if you have them – and how seriously impacted might they be? What will your financial position be if you go on to get divorced?

These are just a few of the huge issues you'd need to consider before making a choice and, as with all difficult decisions, there are many unknowns in the mix. You have a whole raft of information to gather: some of it is emotional, some of it is connected to your family and your wider relationships, and some of it is about your financial situation. Some of the information is clear-cut; much of it is uncertain.

It's important to say, though, that we're not advocating that you should only make a decision when you're forced to. Rather, this is about being clear on the amount of time you have available, and whether using it is going to be to your advantage. So, the question is: do I have time to gather information? And if yes, will gathering information help me make a decision? If the answer to either of these questions is no, you need to speed up your decision-making.

In addition to all that, you're missing out on the potential opportunities that lie on the other side of the post-decision border. Every day that goes by is a lost opportunity to move on, to prepare, to transition; you're stalling, instead of truly living the next phase of your life. And while it is important to think through the consequences of your actions, ask yourself this: are you merely re-making the same decision in your head or recalculating costs you already know outweigh the negatives? If you are getting nothing new from this process and you know the action you want to take, further time investment isn't improving your situation and may be worsening it; it's making you inert, and the more inert we are, the more inert we are likely to continue to be because not doing will become the status quo.

Imagine the following scenario: you and your best friend are out on a hike, somewhere remote and somewhere cold. Now visualise this: you've been walking for four hours. Sunset is at 6pm and it's now 2.30pm. You have warm kit and some snacks, but no head torches and no intention of staying overnight. It's been a beautiful, crisp day – bright but freezing cold. Your friend has said that they know the route (and you're doing a circular walk according to their reckoning) and they've assured you that they know where they are going. Half an hour ago they claimed the route back was less than two hours. But, as you have been walking, you've had an increasing sense that they don't really know where they are going. 'Hey,' you pipe up, 'are you sure this is right . . . we seem to be losing the path. I think we've only got three hours of light left.'

'Erm, yeah, I think so . . . let me check my map,' they reply. 'Yeah . . . this doesn't feel right,' they continue while looking at the map.

What are your thoughts? What do you want to say back and what do you want to do? How are you going to structure how you think about this problem? Take a moment to think it through.

The first question you should think about is time. How much time until sunset? It's now 2.30pm so if you retraced your steps right now you'd spend the last 30 minutes of the walk in fading light. If you can figure out the right route and get back on track you could be back at 4.30pm and you will have completed the walk in two hours with plenty of daylight. However, if you are wrong and you continue to walk in the wrong direction you could get more and more lost. You might, within an hour, still find the path (3.30pm) and then within two hours be back (5.30pm) and thus you'll have completed the remainder of the walk in three hours and still have done it in sunlight.

Of course, lots of things may play into your decision here – your fitness, your friend's fitness, their perceived competence, your ages and your experience. But let's imagine the worst-case scenario here. You and your friend spend too long trying to find the path and then in dwindling light you can't find it and must now spend the night in the freezing cold with no tent, food or source of warmth. You could spend a lot more time looking at the map, checking out short iterations to find the path and then backtracking in the hope that you will firm up whether it is even possible to get back on the right path. But – and here is the crucial question – do you have the time? That should be your starting point since for every minute you spend thinking and checking you are eating into that 30 minutes. Our strong advice would be to say to your friend: 'We can't spend more than 15 minutes assessing our chances and unless within that 15 minutes we can both be 100 per cent certain we are back on the right path we need to go back the way we came.' Why? Because if we wait another 30 minutes we risk losing our least-worst option altogether.

While it is great to ask for more information, firm up hypotheses and get a better picture of what has happened, why it has happened and what will happen, it's even more fundamental to know what impact continued delay causes with regards to our options. We might not like the idea of walking another four hours back in the direction we came, but that option would feel like a very attractive lost opportunity if we found ourselves faced with the worst-worst alternative – hopelessly lost, in the pitch black, freezing cold and facing a night without shelter in the middle of nowhere.

If you're juggling this sort of decision, or indeed even bigger life decisions, and especially if you've been weighing it up for some time, here's the litmus test. Ask yourself the following questions:

- Is there any more information I need to gather?
- Is it possible to gather that information within (a reasonable amount of) time?

In our break-up scenario, you know you'll need to sell the house and divide the proceeds, and you've got a good idea of how much it's worth – this information is gathered. Perhaps you know you're the only partner with a pension, so your other half will be able to claim a part of that – this is more information. But when it comes to your 15-year-old son and 17-year-old daughter, and the fallout your separation will mean to them, where is the information going to come from? You must, as we have seen in Chapter 3, tap into your values; you must use the instinct you have about your children's resilience and mental health. But what you must not do is stall indefinitely; if you do, you'll be failing to use your decision-making power. Because the fact is, you have all the information you can realistically expect to have at this stage. If you delay, you'll be committing neither to trying to make your marriage work, nor to investing in a fresh start on your own or with someone else. And one of these ways forward will be better than the half in/half out position you currently have vis-à-vis your marriage.

The Dangers of Acting Too Soon

One of the questions that long puzzled psychologists was around how the brain factors the passage of time into decision-making. It's quite clear from even a cursory study of human behaviour that the further off a risk or factor is in the future, the greater our ability to downplay it. So we tend to attach more weight to getting a milder illness tomorrow than a more serious one in 20 years' time; and we're more willing to spend money using a credit card, whose repayments we can delay, rather than spending from our current account (despite the fact that this is clearly cheaper, as it doesn't incur interest).

Logically this makes little sense, but researchers have come up with a theory.[3] Over the last several millennia, human brains have evolved in a way that's increased the neural pathways of the posterior area of the ventromedial prefrontal cortex (vmPFC) – one of the areas associated with decision-making – and giving it a lot more connectivity than the anterior region. And it turns out that information around events in the near future is located in the posterior region, while information around events in the future is located in the anterior region. In other words, it seems the brain is primed to respond more effectively to data about the current situation than it is to respond to information about events happening down the line. From an evolutionary point of view, it's easy to understand why that makes sense, but from the point of view of us as human beings with a life expectancy perhaps into our eighties, with the potential for decisions that could affect our quality of life in several decades' time, it makes less sense.

What that may mean in practice is being aware that while our gut instinct might be to act right now, the wiser course of action might be to wait. For example, if you don't get the promotion you'd set your heart on, or if your boss undermines you at work, your first thought might be to jack in the job and walk away from it. In that way, your short-term, i.e. immediate, need for satisfaction will be met.

But at the same time you'll be aware that the wise course of action will be to wait a while; to control the impulse that says 'act now' and pay attention instead to the smaller voice in that anterior region of your vmPFC that's whispering, 'Hang on a minute! Sure, you've got enough money in the bank to manage for a couple of months, but what happens after that?'

Often being 'swept up in the moment' is natural, especially in situations where stress and emotions are high. You will remember in Chapter 3 we talked about the biological response of being placed under stress – our heart starts beating faster, our palms start sweating, and neurologically too, our brain develops tunnel vision on what is right in front of us. Taken together, these are powerful forces working to make us forget about what could come next and focus solely on what's right there for the taking.

But we have to fight this urge. In Chapter 2 we talked about decision inertia and the inability to decide at all, or in time. We discussed the problems of avoidance, redundant deliberation and implementation failure, all of which constitute a slowing of decision-making and the fear to commit to a course of action. Acting too soon is the other side of this coin. We can often be too scared to sit with the discomfort of a decision. This is the problem of choice – choice breeds conflict and it is an unpleasant experience. We do not like having to make choices and we are naturally averse to losses. So the process of weighing up costs and benefits, and working out what we want to sacrifice, is unpleasant. The psychologist Philip Tetlock calls these value-laden decisions 'thinking the unthinkable' because even thinking about some decisions is harmful enough (have I *really* fallen out of love? Am I capable of hurting someone's feelings?).[4] But again, this is why we emphasise the need for bravery and the ability to be open to the decision. Do not fall foul of the tendency to make a quick decision for the sole purpose that either you have a decision to make or that you do not want to be stuck making a decision. This is why we use the Goldilocks analogy so often in our trainings – the opposite of decision inertia is not decision-making that's merely quick, it is decision-making at the right time.

Time urgency

Here's a little exercise we'd like you to do, right now. Put down this book, pick up your phone and start the stopwatch. Wait until you think one minute has elapsed, then go back to your phone and check whether you're early, late or on time with your estimation. Don't count the seconds to make the call: the idea here is to gauge your unconscious instinct on how quickly time passes.

What this shows is something that we have explored at the individual level, and it is the concept of 'time urgency' – the worry that we have about the passage of time, and how aware we are that we are under time pressure. While this may sound like something we should all have in common, it is actually an incredibly diverse individual difference, in which people vary greatly on the degree to which they are 'time urgent'. What's more, time urgency is relatively easy to test.

In a recent study we did, the scores on time urgency ranged from just over 31 seconds (very high time-urgent

people) to over two minutes (very low time-urgent people!).
The lower your score, the more urgency you feel about the
passing concept of time.[5]

Research has found that, in people who are time urgent –
those who believe time passes more quickly than it
does – decision-making ability may be impaired. In one
study, we gave police officers a simulated crime scene and
asked them to hypothesise the possible actions that led to
it.[6] We were interested in both hypothesis quality (was
their idea a good one?) and, more generally, how many
hypotheses the person could come up with for what they
were looking at. Because remember: if you only come up
with one hypothesis, it can lead to closure and faulty
decision-making. It is better to be able to come up with
multiple hypotheses, at least in the early stages of decision-
making. In our study we divided participants into two
groups, and told one group we were 'running a little late'
and that they 'get less time to complete the scenario
compared with other officers'. Despite this, both groups
were actually given the exact same amount of time to do
the study. What we found was that placing people under
time pressure does decrease the quality and quantity of
hypotheses, as you'd expect: but it impacted most on highly
time-urgent individuals, because we were piling our time
pressure on top of their own, innate time pressure. One
theory we have is that in the high time-urgent people, the
knowledge that they (thought) they had less time, coupled
with their pre-existing concerns about how fast time
moved, meant that they wasted an immense amount of

cognitive energy *worrying about time*, and devoted less energy to the process of actually dealing with the problem.

The Law of Diminishing Returns

Acting too quickly may be an immediate instinct, but it's best to overrule it, because even a small pause before making a decision can give you time to gather vital information – a relatively small investment of time into that now could have a huge and disproportionate benefit in terms of your ability to assess the situation you're in and see a clearer pathway through.

But if taking your foot off the pedal is good – and often it is – then it's vital also to remember that, at some point, you need to step back on the gas. That's because, while pausing to get more information makes sense initially, it will eventually cost you more than it advantages you. Again, making a decision is all about making the call about precisely *when* to act.

There's another factor in the mix, which is the law of diminishing returns. It holds that however much a new activity benefits us, the longer we go on doing it, the less effective it will eventually be. This means that while in the early stages a little bit of information can have a huge benefit on our understanding of what is going on and what we can do, this relationship is not equal over time (meaning that often the more and more information we get, the less and less useful it becomes). And chasing that information can often result in us simply falling into the trap of decision inertia that we described in Chapter 2.

Let's take our divorce decision outlined earlier in this chapter. In many cases, spending some time really thinking about the options financially, socially and emotionally is incredibly important – especially when there are kids involved – and it can help avoid the emotionally driven impulse decision after a particularly bad argument. But at the same time, it can be easy to fall into the habit of constantly wanting to think more and want more, going down rabbit holes of information gathering and 'what if' thinking about faraway conundrums (who will our yet-to-be-born grandchildren spend Christmas with?) that can prevent you from making the decision that is right in front of you. This is why after you have asked yourself if you have time to gather more information, do not forget to ask yourself whether the information you are getting is really helping, or whether it is simply giving you an excuse to avoid the decision.

This is why the idea of time is so important, because it is not simply that the more time you have/use, the better. What we often find is that a little bit of time investment in the early phases has an immensely important benefit on how well we can make decisions. Often when we make errors in decision-making we find out that there were a few pieces of information that could have easily been found out had we just spent additional time searching. It is not simply about spending additional time confirming, or additional time planning, what we are going to do. We have to use the little time that we have wisely to *probe* what is going on.

Foxtrot thinking

By looking at not just the decision-making *outcomes* of expert decision makers but the time patterns that they commonly adopt – how long they spend assessing the situation, choosing a course of action and committing themselves to that decision – we have discovered that the ideal approach is what we term 'foxtrot thinking': slow, slow; quick, quick.

What we mean by this is that you start by taking time to carefully assess the different options, to call on any relevant experience of the sort of situation you're facing and on your internal value system. This is the 'slow, slow' stage that we covered in Chapters 3 and 4 – the information you will assemble here will pay enormous dividends in helping you make the right choice.

But once this information is assembled, and any further information will either take too long to find or will never be available, you need to move into the 'quick, quick' phase. The law of diminishing returns means the information you found quickly at the start is likely to dry up, from which point you're going to be investing time that isn't rewarded by turning up anything new or significant. This is what we call 'redundant deliberation', and it means people are taking too long to decide what to do, because they're hoping they can get more information. It's connected also to a tendency to maximise or, in other words, to wait for a more 'perfect' solution to emerge – and, as we've already seen in Chapter 3, that is rarely helpful. Added to which, some individuals display what psychologists call a 'need for closure' (which we'll cover in the next chapter), which means they struggle to deal with uncertainty. In these people, the passage of time becomes inextricably linked to the problem itself and may even become more burdensome, since they're worrying as much about time passing as they are about the need to make a choice.

Our own research into how police officers make decisions bears out our theory on foxtrot thinking. In a study involving 96 senior police officers, recruited from across the UK, we found that those with military experience – i.e. individuals who had studied good decision-making in the field and had plenty of experience of it – tended to take more time to assess a situation, but less time to decide on a course of action.[7]

Setting Deadlines: Being Clear On *When* to Act

Let's end this chapter with an example that helps us see the role of time in action. It may seem like a straightforward example, and a long way from the high-stakes decisions we outlined earlier in this chapter, but we hope it will illustrate the point. Imagine that you are in a taxi going from central London to Euston station. You are about to get a train that is a four-hour journey back home. It is a hot summer day. Your train is at 12pm and you are very eager to get home, having worked very hard for the last three days. The time now is 11.35am, so you have 25 minutes for the cab to get you to Euston. However, there is a problem: you're stuck in very heavy traffic. The taxi is nudging forward very slowly and you are starting to get concerned that you will miss your train. You're thinking to yourself, 'Maybe this traffic will speed up in a minute and I can zoom into Euston and grab a coffee. I'll have a good ten minutes before I need to get on that train.' On the other hand, if you don't move forward fairly soon you're definitely going to miss that train. You do know that you could stop the cab now, pay and leave, and you would have 20 minutes to get to Euston. That would mean you walking at a very brisk pace, but nonetheless you know that you would get there on time. You'd likely end up not being able to grab that coffee and you'd likely be puffed and out of breath. So, here's the decision: do you chance the cab will get you there in time and perhaps the jam will clear in the next minute or so and then it'll only take three minutes to get you there? Or do you make the decision to walk at a really fast pace, miss that coffee, suffer a very uncomfortable, sweaty ride home looking rather dishevelled, be out of breath, but at least make the train – just about? What would you do?

In terms of time, there are a few 'errors' you could make. You could decide too early, jump out of the cab and begin to walk, only to then have the cab drive right past you a minute later. You could decide too late, and effectively miss your window to even get out of the cab and start the walk. Your indecision in this case would have removed the choice from you. Instead you know that you have a finite window to act if you want to make your train.

This brings up a second question: what do you actually want to do? You can spend the next five minutes agonising over the traffic patterns, potential detours, looking to see if the lanes are speeding up and ruminating on what you *could* do. But without identifying what your actual goal is, you are unlikely to escape this incident happy. What are your values? Are you in a hurry? Do you need to get home or are you happy to get the next train? Is there something you are desperate to get home for (your partner, your child)? Or has it just been a long day and you want to get home, but you also really don't want to sit on a train sweaty and uncomfortable all for the sake of 'not missing it'? If you value the former – and it's a 25-minute walk – the minute the clock hits 27 minutes from departure you need to get out of the cab (no matter where it is) because it is the *only* way to *guarantee* that you get home. If there is nothing at home for you, then accept you might not make your train, embrace the fact you will be comfortable and hydrated (you might even have time for a nice meal) and relax. You will make it home eventually.

While this is an example of an everyday rather than a tumultuous decision, it illustrates the need to know what matters to you. It shows how what we recommend, which is tapping into your values, helps you set the compass on your decisions. Because even in the back of that cab, with something as small-scale as which train you're going to catch, anchoring your decision in what matters to you makes it much easier to decide what to do.

DECISION TIME TIPS

1. Be brave and do not feel the need to do anything right away. Embrace the fact that you have a decision to make and that 'making it quickly' may lead to less happiness in the long run.

2. Before making any critical decision, ask the very simple question: 'Do I need to decide now?' For most of us and most of the time the answer will likely be 'no'. Very bad decisions can most certainly be made too early due to a desire to create immediate resolution. Firing off an immediate response email is almost always a very bad idea. Recognise that impulsivity stands in the way of getting a good idea of the scenario (what has happened, why it has happened and what may happen next).

3. If you don't need to decide now, think about constructing a reasonable and proportionate time frame. Very often there is not a specific externally imposed deadline and the decision therefore drifts and drifts, making avoidance and inertia even more likely. Of course, every decision is different and so the time frame may be different, but failing to impose a deadline will mean continued delay. A good clue as to whether you are in a delay trap of constantly asking for more information is that with each new acquisition of information it seems less and less useful to guide you. The diminishing returns on the utility of

information is a good clue that you are in a redundant deliberation loop!

4. On the rare occasion that you do need to decide now then you need to think 'least worst first'. Why? Because if you wait too long the least-worst option may disappear, leaving you with the inevitable consequence of the worst of the worst.

CHAPTER 6

Adaptation

J ACK WASN'T LOOKING for another job, but when the headhunter called he was flattered – 'Hey! They think I can head up this big new sales team!' – and the more he thought about it, the more interested he became. There had been a few issues at work recently: his new boss was piling too much on him and he was fed up with failures to do with his team not carrying through actions they'd all agreed on in meetings.

He met up with the recruitment consultant and then with one of the partners from the new firm. The post they were looking to fill would involve about three nights a week in London, and Jack lived in Yorkshire: he'd be away from early Tuesday to late Thursday. A bit of an issue, he thought, but his wife Connie would enjoy some quiet time with the kids, who were five and seven. Talking to the partner raised a couple of questions in his mind about the purpose and value of the merchandise the company was selling, but he glossed over it. This was a big opportunity – an opportunity he hadn't even had to hustle for! He was getting away from a difficult boss and a troublesome team, and he couldn't wait to get his feet under his new desk.

Jack made his move, but a year later, he quit his new job even though he hadn't got another sorted out. The new company wasn't right for him: he didn't fit in there and, in his heart, he didn't value what it was selling. Being away from his family had put his marriage under enormous strain: Connie resented having to do the lion's share of the childcare, and they both missed being together. Jack had found himself sitting in his lonely hotel room thinking how he'd much rather be at home. Eventually, Connie gave him an ultimatum: his marriage or his job. Jack handed in his notice, and a few weeks later found a lower paid and less prestigious job an hour's commute from their house.

The story didn't end in disaster: Jack learned from his mistakes and he and Connie realised how much being together meant to them. But the wrong move could have been avoided if he'd been what we term more 'fluid' in his thinking around making his decision: because when you dissect the choice Jack made, he cut off too many possibilities, too early on. From the moment the headhunter approached him, he allowed himself to feel flattered and excited about the idea of the new job, and from that very first call he decided it was for him. As a result, the alarm bells that should have been loud and clear were muted; he saw what he wanted to see and ignored the potential stumbling blocks.

Jack might have found it helpful to spend some time pondering on whether he could have improved the glitches in his old workplace. Sure, that headhunter made him realise how several elements of his old post weren't suiting him anymore, but with hindsight, it would have been better if he'd at least considered whether he could have improved his lot there, rather than moving on. Would a chat to his boss have improved their working relationship? Were there changes he could have made to his team to make them more effective? And if the old job wasn't fixable, might Jack have been able to find a more compatible role if he'd looked elsewhere for it, rather than focusing on the opportunity the headhunter had given him?

Jack's error was to move, much too quickly, to a situation where he could only see one option – in this case, an option he hadn't worked out for himself but had been presented with. From the very start, he focused on the 'opportunity' rather than on the other signals and the wider picture: right through the process, he selected the pieces of information that shored up his decision to jump ship for the new job and toned down what should have been niggling doubts that made him re-evaluate whether this really would work for him and his family.

We are now in the middle of our STAR model – you have assessed the situation and what you are dealing with, and you have assessed how much time you have and when you need to make a decision, but now comes the tricky part of using the right strategies and techniques to make the decision. Too often we see novices fall foul of cognitive fallacies that give the illusion of the 'right' answer without recognising the need to dig deeper. In this chapter we teach you how to avoid these fallacies, how to engage in the right cognitive processes, at the right time, and how to eventually make sure that you are committing to the right decision for the right reasons. First, let's look at some of the pitfalls we need you to avoid.

Cognitive Closure

Being able to adapt is crucial to effective decision-making, which is why it's the third principle in our 'STAR' model. Psychologists have known for a long time that personality plays a huge role here, because of a particular trait that influences a person's ability to demonstrate fluid thinking – a trait that's linked to the fact that evolution has programmed us to very strongly prefer certainty over uncertainty. Consequently, we have an inbuilt code that gives us a tendency to what psychologists call 'seeking closure'. What that means is, we naturally strive to work out how something will progress, so we can be 'sure' about what's going on and work out what we believe is going to happen next. We lean towards finding answers, even at the risk of ignoring the questions that might lead to the right answers.

To show the power of this process, let's do a quick test. Read the following words:

S _ _ R
T_ M _
CH _ _ _ E

Did your mind immediately fill in the blanks and let you imagine a complete word? We feel better filling in the uncertainty with information, even though there is no way to be sure which word it is (did you go for star or scar, time or tame, choice or change?). This is just a snippet of the human need to fill in the blanks in all facets of life – but critically when trying to work out what is going on and what we are going to do.

The concept of a need for closure (NFC) was developed in the 1990s by the US social psychologist Arie Kruglanski, and it holds that some people prize certainty so highly that they shy away from situations that introduce them to the 'grey' areas of life.[1] For them, everything is clear-cut; right or wrong, correct or incorrect. What that means in the context of decision-making, though, is that possibilities that might be very helpful – even essential – are overlooked or, worse, ignored. Or even – worse still – pieces of information that point quite clearly in one direction are engineered within the mind of a person with a high NFC to fit the picture required.

Taken to the extreme, this way of thinking can lead to disaster, and one example of that, much studied by Kruglanski, was the Egyptian-Syrian attack launched against Israel on 6 October 1973, triggering the Yom Kippur War that left many thousands dead and Israel – despite eventual military victory – sorely bruised.

For Kruglanski, the most interesting element of the war was that the Arab attack on Israel was totally unexpected, despite the existence of a whole raft of worrying indicators collected by Israeli intelligence (AMAN) and other bodies. When he explored further, he discovered that two key Israeli leaders had an especially high NFC, which led them to 'freeze' whenever evidence was presented that the Arabs might be planning to attack. They believed the Arabs didn't have the suitable weapons for an Israeli attack, and that it would be at least five years before things changed – and as evidence started to mount that this was mistaken, they simply closed their minds to it.

Worse still, according to Kruglanski, they shut down voices arguing against them: at one point, one of them told his subordinate officers that those who argued an Arab assault was likely could wave goodbye to promotion. Even as the war was starting, these men argued that the mistake wasn't theirs – it was the Egyptian leader's. While this pattern of ignoring information that might seem to 'second-guess' our current perception may seem strange, in his study of US presidential decisions, the British-American academic David Houghton identified this non-ideal form of thinking as a factor in the decision to increase the number of troops in Vietnam, the attempted coup of Cuba (referred to as the 'Bay of Pigs' disaster) and the Cuban missile crisis.[2]

According to Kruglanski, the need for cognitive closure plays a key function in judgement-forming processes by bringing the information processing to a halt. He identified two varieties of NFC: non-specific (i.e. the need for any closure) and specific (i.e. the need for a particular form of closure). With colleagues, Kruglanski devised a test that indicates whether individuals have a high or low NFC.

There are different versions of the test but, to get a sense of where you are in relation to this construct, think about the extent to which you agree with the 15 statements below. You can use the following scale to get a more precise version and write it against each sentence or simply tot up your scores in your head:

> 1 = Strongly disagree, 2 = Moderately disagree,
> 3 = Slightly disagree, 4 = Slightly agree,
> 5 = Moderately agree, 6 = Strongly agree

Once you have finished, add up your total score.

1. I don't like situations that are uncertain.

2. I dislike questions that could be answered in many different ways.

3. I find that a well-ordered life with regular hours suits my temperament.

4. I feel uncomfortable when I don't understand the reason why an event occurred in my life.

5. I feel irritated when one person disagrees with what everyone else in a group believes.

6. I don't like to go into a situation without knowing what I can expect from it.

7. When I have made a decision, I feel relieved.

8. When I am confronted with a problem, I'm dying to reach a solution very quickly.

9. I would quickly become impatient and irritated if I could not find a solution to a problem immediately.

10. I don't like to be with people who are capable of unexpected actions.

11. I dislike it when a person's statement could mean many different things.

12. I find that establishing a consistent routine enables me to enjoy life more.

13. I enjoy having a clear and structured mode of life.

14. I do not usually consult many different opinions before forming my own view.

15. I dislike unpredictable situations.

Now, imagine a bell curve across a scale of 0–70. At the bottom end (roughly 0–15) are those who have an incredibly low need for closure. They are not motivated at all to seek certainty and embrace openness. In the middle (15–55) we have those individuals who vary slightly on a range from enjoying some openness to a slight need for certainty. The majority of people who take this test will fall into this category. Finally, 55–70 is those with an extremely high need for closure. They are incredibly motivated for closure and they will often simplify complex problems to ensure that there is absolutely no uncertainty.

Perhaps unsurprisingly Laurence scored bang on 30 and so would be considered as well below average on NFC and thus unlikely to, as Kruglanski would say, 'seize' too rapidly on an idea or 'freeze' and thus be unable to adjust to new information and form a different view based on new evidence. Neil scored much lower than 30, and is therefore even more willing to embrace (even seek out) uncertainty. And this is not a bad thing. Think about this book. The story we told you in Chapter 1 was that the predominant view (and even theories) of decision-making is that people are rational and that they use known information to make choices between a finite number of choices. These are then tested with different paradigms in the laboratory. From 'gambling tasks' to 'shopping tasks', most of the research on decision-making is centred on certainty. We, on the other hand, disagree and indeed have searched out uncertainty. We don't want to know how people make decisions in closed, certain environments (we think this is relatively boring), we want to know how people make open, uncertain, incredibly hard decisions when uncertainty is at its highest. It is probably to a degree our own relationship with uncertainty that leads us on the quest to explore how people handle similar situations – and in doing so, to write a book trying to help you deal with uncertainty when you face it (even if you are high in NFC!). But people vary in NFC, and indeed our own samples vary greatly. Of course, some people can score very high on some items and very low on others thus resulting in the same average score as someone scoring each individual item straight down the middle. More on this in a moment, but for now just concentrate on what high (over 55) or low (below 15) might mean.

Having a high NFC is one important way in which human beings tend to narrow their decision-making propensity. If you score over 55 you are the sort of person who, when making arrangements, wants to know the time, the place, what you are going to eat, what is happening afterwards, who will be there, and so on. You'll also likely want to know the arrangements as soon as possible rather than at the last minute. Having someone with really low NFC make arrangements for a party of people with high NFC would cause the invitees considerable stress. Having someone with really high NFC make arrangements for invitees with low NFC may also lead to stress since the invitees would now feel like the event was very formal and any breach would be seen as a major infraction. I (Neil) remember recently a stag do ('bachelor party' in the United States) in which the best man (and planner in chief) was incredibly high NFC and had the itinerary planned down to the five-minute mark, including departure and arrival times based on the commute. When the rest of the party took too long, deviated or generally made up plans on the spot, it caused him immense stress and indeed everyone else immense enjoyment. That said, it is not that low NFC people never get anxious. I (Laurence) should note that, despite my very low NFC, even I was mildly anxious when I did some work for a special forces team in London and was simply told that my workshop was in London in the morning, but had no time, no location or no indication of how long I was talking for. The special forces guys dealing with that particular situation were obviously low NFC as well.

As with all things, there are some advantages to a low NFC but also some disadvantages when it comes to critical incident decision-making. Think about these and how they may apply to you.

Scoring low means you can tolerate ambiguity. Situations that are uncertain are going to cause you less stress. That means while you are developing your situational awareness of what has happened, why it is happening and what may happen next, you can hold in your mind two or three options more comfortably for longer. You'll likely be more resistant to having to pin one of them down too quickly (seizing). If you are very high NFC you may think 'It could be any one of these three options, but I must immediately find out which of the three or I'll continue to be stressed out.' You may also find it harder and more stressful to adjust in light of new information: 'Damn, this new information suggests I might be wrong about what I thought was happening, but, screw it, let's just stick with what I thought the situation was because it's easier.' That said, if you are really low on NFC you might be the sort of person who is so comfortable not knowing which of the three it is that you spend too long luxuriating in not knowing. And, as we have seen, sometimes we have to act faster than that.

This is where in our own work we have discovered that the different factors within NFC play a role in critical incident decision-making. In the full version of Kruglanski's scale there are subfactors within NFC that are important to think about. These are:

- The need for order versus low need for order.
- The need for predictability versus low need for predictability.
- Indecisiveness versus decisiveness.
- The avoidance of ambiguity versus tolerance for ambiguity.
- Closed-mindedness versus open-mindedness.

Obviously the more inclined you are towards needing order, predictability and decisiveness, the higher your NFC. But, what if someone scored very high on some of these factors (i.e. they were highly decisive but were tolerant of ambiguity)? They'd be average on NFC, but that does not mean they would be average in making critical decisions. In fact, what we found was that, depending on the combination of scores, they could be really outstanding.[3] Specifically, and with respect to a study we did on police officers investigating very difficult sexual assault cases, we found that individuals with the combination of high decisiveness (high NFC) and tolerance of ambiguity (low NFC) and thus generating an average NFC score (high + low = average) did extremely well in complex sexual assault cases.[4] And this makes sense doesn't it . . . an investigator should be open-minded and able to deal with complex ambiguous information, but also very decisive.

As with much of what we have highlighted, most extreme scores on any psychological construct can be problematic since an extreme makes you adept in some very specific circumstances but fragile in others. And, as we have pointed out, managing the most critical events in life means acting neither too quickly nor too slowly and being able to adjust accordingly. This Goldilocks maxim of neither too hot nor too cold but just right is how you can conceptualise decision-making: not too much situational awareness, not too fast or slow to make a decision, and not too much or too little analysis or information searching.

Even if you do have some extreme attributes, all is not lost. Being aware of your tendencies and personality type is the most important thing of all. We all have strengths and weaknesses, advantages and disadvantages, positives and negatives – and indeed, as we have seen, something that's a strength in one area of life can be a weakness in another. So what's crucial is to know how you function as an individual, so you can be ready to override the shortcomings you may have where decision-making is concerned.

Cognitive Tricks and Treats

NFC is not the only human tendency that can be problematic when it comes to making good choices. In addition to the fact that our personality works to try to control and minimise uncertainty, our mind is primed to adopt cognitive tricks to try to help us find closure.

Much of this stems from the scale and complexities of the world in which we find ourselves, and in which we must make our decisions. There are a plethora of causes and effects for any life event, interacting within a single situation; and indeed all situations can be viewed as intertwined. But it's important to tease apart the threads so you can explain what has happened, what is happening and (crucially) what is going to happen next, while acknowledging that this involves trying to comprehend an immensely complex system of interactions and factors within a single (manageable) perspective.

It's quite the task.

The problem is: our brains are not up to that task. In many cases we cannot comprehend all the moving parts and the plethora of possible and multiple futures. We cannot grasp complex causality and the immense interrelations that exist. Instead we have to be, as the psychologist Herbert A. Simon put it in 1956, 'cognitive misers' who dole out cognitive effort as minimally as possible.[5] In fact, rather than being evolved to maximise our interpretation of complex situations and systems, we seem to be evolved to minimise our interpretation of complexity, and instead often adopt simple 'rules' and 'heuristics' that help us see past complexity and attempt to see the simple underlying rules that govern the world. The problem, however, is that while these rules and heuristics do achieve the goal of simplifying our world view, they often do so at the cost of accuracy and good decision-making.

Back in the 1970s the legendary psychologists Amos Tversky and Daniel Kahneman did a lot of work on how we simplify information to help us make choices.[6] Their thesis was that people rely on a limited number of possibilities, and that they make assumptions that, though generally helpful, will sometimes undermine the entire process. For example, if Event A usually generates Event B, we will tend to make our decisions assuming that this is the pattern events will take, but that is only a probability, and every so often Event C will follow Event A.

What fascinated Tversky and Kahneman were the ways in which the mind plays tricks that affect our judgement; and what they discovered was that, however smart we are and however much we know this isn't the case, we inherently tend to assume that things will be the way we have known or seen them. For example, if we see a crash on the motorway, we will feel we are more likely to be involved in one ourselves, even though the fact of having seen it makes no difference to our own odds. Or another example: child abduction is extremely rare, but a police officer who has worked on a case of child abduction recently is more likely to worry that their own children might become victims, although the risk for any individual child is minuscule.

In all sorts of ways, Tversky and Kahneman discovered, the human mind plays strange tricks to lead us to make assumptions that have little basis in probability. Worse, we're likely to have the most confidence in the least accurate predictions. Decision-making could be much improved, they argued, if human beings understood that they were imbued with these biases – so they could override them, rather than blithely allowing them to undermine good judgement.

Fortunately, there are many tactics you can use to help override these go-to heuristics that can sometimes lead us down an easier cognitive path but, ultimately, to the wrong destination.

Overcoming the odds

The next time you've developed your assessment of the situation and feel pretty confident in it – and, crucially, you have the time to test it – think about the following:

- Seek the opposite: don't simply look for information to confirm what you think. In Jack's case this was looking for all the reasons why he should take the job. Actively seek out information that challenges your preferred view. So, Jack should imagine all the reasons he shouldn't take the job.

- All information matters: don't assume the first piece of information you find is the most informative. We are all subject to what psychologists call 'primacy effects', where we value the first piece of information more than any subsequent pieces. If Jack thought the job looked good at first because it had a higher salary than his current job, but then found out that after tax and with hotel costs and travel he would only be on a fraction more than he was on now, that new information should count. Equally, don't think the final piece of information is the most useful just because it was the last piece of the puzzle. For example, Jack has now looked at all the information and he decides perhaps he won't take the job, but then suddenly the employer says 'I'll cover all your hotel fees.' Wow! Suddenly that problem is solved – so Jack should rush to take the job? No, not unless he has really thought through the full picture. This is only one of the issues – it doesn't, for example, change anything on the family front.

- If it's not black and white, it's not black and white: sometimes we have a tendency to reduce a problem to an either/or: 'My stocks took a dive so I must sell', 'My team isn't good enough to win the championship so I must leave', 'I am unhappy in my relationship so I should go.' Life can be, but is not always, that simple; so it's often worth looking for a third or even fourth way. In Jack's case because he was unhappy with his current job anything looked better – especially the shiny new one. Because of his need for speed he thought enough neither about the limitations of the shiny new job nor the potential ways in which he might be able to improve the new one.

- Take advice from friends (and, sometimes, enemies): good decision-making is often aided by being able to cross-check your ideas and your information with others. Do this across a range of people and not just the ones you favour. Indeed, even someone you don't like or who hasn't given you much help in the past may have something useful to say. Don't judge the information on the basis of who has said it or even how or why they said it. Just think about what they have said – and remember, even a broken clock is right twice a day.

- Interrogate your information: there are at least three ways in which you should do this: do you have the full picture (or are there gaps); is some of the information inconsistent and contradictory;

and have you tested what you assume to be true? If not then you should seek to plug the gaps (find out more), resolve the inconsistencies and test the assumptions. Remember, though, that this seeking more information should be a finite process and there is a trade-off between accuracy and time.

Analogies and anecdotes

One of the final issues that we need to overcome is the failure to adapt our decision-making process. In the first chapter we presented the tri-modal theory of decision-making (page 25) – the idea that there are three different strategies for making decisions: follow the rules, learn from past experience or make a choice. One of the things that we often see is that people believe that they can just follow the rules, or believe that they can just use their experience, but in actuality they cannot. Trying to apply the wrong kind of decision-making process may be one of the worst pitfalls of all!

As we've already seen, one of the simplest decision rules can be roughly defined as 'What did I do the last time I faced this decision, and did it work?' If the answer is 'yes', do it again. If the answer is 'no', do something else. Such a strategy is incredibly useful and, indeed, in many cases can help us quickly and effectively make the right decision: 'Last time I was running late for work and took the highway through the city, there was a traffic jam and I was 30 minutes late for my meeting. This time, I'll take the ring road', 'Last time I took a risk and tried a large jump ramp, I broke my leg and needed surgery. This time, I will stick to the piste', 'Last time I travelled across the world for a first date, it was a massive failure. This time, I'll call first.' But what about when you think that you are facing 'the same decision again', but it is in fact completely different? If you simply think 'I'll do what I did last time', you will lose the opportunity to fully develop the story and miss what is really going on.

Let's take a hypothetical work scenario that you may have faced yourselves. Imagine that you are working at your company and you get turned down for a promotion or a project. You feel slighted, but your boss tells you to wait, because they have a really big project coming in six months that they want you to lead. 'Oh I've heard this before,' you may think. At your last job your boss kept promising the next opportunity was just round the corner, only it never materialised and you wasted another 18 months at the company before you finally left. 'Not this time,' you think – and you learn from your mistakes and begin to look at the job ads.

But, hang on a minute, what if this situation is not like the last? What if this boss is telling you the truth? What if your analogy of the situation, while it may have seemed right at the time, could have easily been falsified? Perhaps the company has recently got a lot of new business (and your last company was struggling). What if your boss has always appeared to value you and given you glowing reviews and told you that they have a plan for your long-term development? Are these indicators not signs that this situation is *different*, and that therefore your initial analogy may be wrong?

Psychologists have called this tendency 'analogical decision-making' and it involves using analogies between past events and the present to help you predict what will happen if you take a given decision. Analogies are incredibly powerful decision-making tools – they can, if used correctly, bring a lot of new knowledge to an uncertain situation by allowing us to use what we learned last time we faced a similar situation. But this model of decision-making, despite its immense prevalence in how we navigate the world, only works if the situations we face are total (or close to total) reruns of a previous situation. While many situations are repeatable – buying coffee, going to the gym – it is very unlikely that we have experienced the exact same situation time and time again. And, crucially, even a tiny bit of difference in a scenario can change everything.

It is one of the common tropes in movies, and unfortunately in the decisions of those around us, that we often see people applying the wrong analogies and thinking that they are constantly facing the *same* situations time and time again when they are not. In these cases, they are using the wrong decision-making strategy. They are making analogies, based on history, and not taking a moment to think about whether this situation is new and, as such, requires a fresh set of processes: situational awareness, choice, value identification (as we saw in Chapter 3). We have to know when to stop just doing what we did last time. One of the examples we often use to show the problem of inaccurately using analogies is the decision-making of former US president Barack Obama when he had to decide how to deal with the emerging Syrian civil war in Syria, 2011. This was no easy decision: on every front, there was the chance of disaster. The decision was a classic least-worst problem: no decision guaranteed success, and every day action was delayed there was a greater cost to human life. To date, the total number of deaths in the Syrian civil war is over 500,000.

When this decision was unfolding in front of us in the summer of 2011 we wanted to get a sense of how the president was handling the situation and how he was making his decisions. The way he was making decisions was often discussed publicly, so we could glean an insight into how he was interpreting the situation, the unfolding situational awareness, their potential plans and when they thought they may act. We reviewed over 438 documents – from speeches to press remarks – which included over 4,700 mentions of Syria and the Syrian civil war.

What was clear from the analysis was the way in which Obama was using analogies to guide his thinking. This is not surprising and is indeed a tactic most presidents, like most people, have tended to use. But in all cases, the analogies of previous experiences were from different countries: and the situation faced in Syria was not the same as that faced in Iraq, or Libya, or even Afghanistan in the 1980s. In the end, the US did nothing – and while it is impossible to know the outcomes of any action, it is hard to imagine a worse outcome than what has happened there since.

The lesson here is a simple lesson of adaptation. Often in life you will face decisions that look and feel familiar.

But, all the same, you need to ask yourself whether history truly is repeating itself. And, as we outlined in the previous chapters, you should not look for evidence to *confirm* that history is repeating itself, but evidence of *if* history is repeating itself. Courage is required: you need to be ready to embrace the fact that if this is not something you have experienced before – a unique experience – then you have to be prepared to adapt and accept that you cannot take the cognitively easy way out.

You are going to have to make a choice.

But, and this is the good news, knowing that you are facing a choice and making it is a far better outcome than *thinking* you are facing a situation you have faced before and not even embracing the process of choice.

DECISION TIME TIPS

1. Train your mind to think more clearly and rationally, and to make logical connections between ideas. We certainly know that thinking usefully is about more than having knowledge; it's about understanding the weight we apportion to different elements of whatever we're assessing, and readjusting some of them in the light of self-knowledge.

- Practise contra-logical thinking: 'What would happen if I do this?', 'Would I think differently if [a given variable] was changed in this situation?'

- Know your tendencies. Having a high NFC is not something simply to be aware of; it's something you can influence by making conscious changes to your thinking patterns and behaviour. Pay attention to how you approach things: just because a certain methodology has always worked for you, don't assume it always will, or that it's not worth trying a different way of looking at something. Try to think about things from another point of view or a different angle; try to imagine yourself in someone else's shoes and see whether it alters the way you look at something. Are you seeking closure for the sake of closure? Are you embracing uncertainty, at the cost of needing closure? Like maximisation in Chapter 3, what matters is knowing your tendencies, and when you need to lean into them and when you need to rein them in.
- Identify your biases (remember: you need to be aware of biases to override them) and focus on the difference between inference and assumptions. Be alert to common thinking errors: don't allow your thought processes to become clouded by illusions and misconceptions.

2. Be critical when you think you have 'experienced' something before. Have you looked for evidence that it is the same as the last time or have you looked for evidence that confirms it is the same as the last time? These are two different things.

3. Be prepared to adapt your approach. Know when to abandon previous analogies if they do not seem right. Embrace a unique opportunity – if it goes wrong, after all, you have a new experience to learn from. But do not make the mistake of thinking you have been here before when you haven't.

4. Be bold and embrace the complexity of choice. Using analogies is cognitively easier and may not require the depth of thought that a new choice does, but the rewards are worthwhile if you follow your values.

CHAPTER 7

Redirecting the Trolley

A S A PROFESSOR at the University of Massachusetts Lowell, I (Neil) recently worked with a young undergraduate called Tyler. We met as part of an internship in which we were recruited by Facebook and the Department of Homeland Security to develop an online programme that could help prevent young people from being swayed by the pulls of online extremism. At the time, over 250 young Americans (and even more Europeans) had fled their home countries and joined the terrorist group the Islamic State. Tyler had the idea of launching an educational platform to teach basic online safety to young children across the country. So, with a group of four fellow students, he launched 'Operation250' and began the process of trying to get his programme up and running. Several months into this journey, while Tyler's programme was doing well, it was not providing him with much of a livelihood. He lived on friends' couches, in a range of relatively unsavoury (but cheap) rentals, and even (at one point) in his car. He lived off a diet of pasta. Fast forward 12 months and Tyler's programme has received over

$1,000,000 in funding. He was awarded a prestigious award from the State of Massachusetts for his effort and his programme was featured by the United Nations Educational, Scientific and Cultural Organization's handbook on youth-led efforts to counter violent extremism. Most importantly, he can provide for himself and is living the life of a young entrepreneur and CEO of his own company.

Tyler's story represents what is common among many stories of success – perseverance and not giving up when a decision we've made doesn't seem to be going our way. It is a story we hear all of the time: NASA experienced 20 failures in its 28 attempts to send rockets to space; Henry Ford's early businesses failed and left him broke five times before he founded Ford Motor Company; it took Thomas Edison 1,000 attempts before inventing the light bulb (his teachers also told him growing up that he was too stupid to learn anything); Dr Seuss's first book was rejected by 27 publishers before it was accepted; Michael Jordan was cut from his high-school *basketball team* for not being good enough. In all of these cases, the person at the centre persisted. Despite difficulty, despite failure, despite all evidence to the contrary, they knew when to keep going.

On the other hand, we have also all heard of success stories where people realise that their current path is not bringing them the happiness that they long for in their life and they decide to make a drastic (and often risky) change. Ray Kroc, the man who created the McDonald's empire, spent his career as a milkshake-device salesman before buying McDonald's at the age of 52 in 1954. Vera Wang, now one of the world's premier designers, was a figure skater and journalist before entering the fashion industry at the age of 40. Ronald Reagan, the fortieth president of the United States, spent the majority of his life as an actor in Hollywood. And before launching the now-viral new media site BuzzFeed (the one that often predicts what *Friends* character you would be based on your breakfast order) and The Huffington Post, Jonah Peretti was a middle-school teacher who taught Microsoft Office. In all of these cases, these people were able to give up the status quo and make a drastic decision without any evidence that their new-found plans and career change would lead to success.

It is easy to talk about success stories, but we often forget to talk about the far more common cases of people who either do not persist enough or persist too much. You may know individuals like this – many of us do. It's that friend who is the funniest person you know and makes everyone laugh, but never takes that next step on to the stage at a comedy club. Or the friend who loves fitness and health, has even started their own Instagram page of training tips, but lacks the courage to follow that dream in their professional life. We all know someone who we know has great potential and a gift to share with the world, but they are too afraid to embrace the potential of failure and see it through. They hear the first bit of negative feedback and allow it to defeat them. Or, worse, their fear of negative feedback prevents them from even trying.

This is the final part of our decision-making STAR model: knowing when to stay the course and knowing when to redirect the trolley. It's the 'R', for revision. To make decisions that are energy-giving and can truly shape our lives, we need to be able to identify the factors that so often keep us rooted to the spot, refusing to accept that our current career, relationship, diet, behaviour – whatever it may be – will not achieve the goals we are looking for, and the factors that make us unable to overcome difficulties and maintain the course when the going gets tough. We need to keep our lives, our motives, our values and, most of all our living-out of them, under constant surveillance; because it's keeping them at the heart of ourselves, being honest about ourselves about what matters to us and being willing to make the changes that will align our behaviour with our values, that sound decision-making is based on.

Avoiding Change

When we know we need to change, what stops us from making the change?

The fact is, we're psychologically programmed to prefer things to remain as they are. It's a fascinating element of how the human mind works, and it's deeply engrained and much researched. But we'd like to encourage you to override the instinctive human brake system, because if things aren't working, you have everything to gain if you take action.

Let's start off by examining what psychological research has discovered about how our brains work when it comes to embracing, or avoiding, change.

Status quo bias

At the heart of our attitude to change is something we've already touched on: it's around our deepest human fear, which is loss. Because change will inevitably involve loss as well as gain – even if we have good reason to hope for a positive outcome. The losses are always clamouring in our heads for airtime, and we seem to be programmed to give them the most attention. Fascinatingly, research has suggested there's a neurological reason for this.[1] It seems that the brain processes gains in its 'reward section' – that's the part of the brain that's activated, for example, by us enjoying food when we're hungry or getting an unexpected pay bonus. But losses are processed in the part of the brain that's reserved for strong negative reactions, such as disgust or pain. Those are the last bits of our brain that we want to engage with, and this research hints at how far we're prepared to go to avoid it – even failing to follow up on plans that could give us huge gains.

And there's more. Not only do we fear loss above all else, we also have a special fear reserved for losses we believe we've caused ourselves. And that in turn has given us a tendency to believe that harmful actions are worse than harmful inactions. In essence, we seem to have been designed to play life 'safe' or, better yet, 'let things be'. Whatever we say out loud about the benefits of change, in our deepest selves we don't want to risk the pain of the change going wrong. The idea of preferring inaction and the subsequent negative outcomes over proactively initiating an action that causes a loss is exemplified in what has become known as 'the trolley problem'.

Let's say you work for a transport company in which you operate the lines for a trolleybus that moves people from A to B. You control two tracks – a north track and a north east track – on which you operate a one-tonne trolley that carries around 80 people. You have access to CCTV that enables you to see if anyone is on the tracks. The trolley can't be stopped, only redirected. Currently it's heading north.

You see when you check the CCTV that there is a child on the north east track. You're going to need to try to sort that out, but thank goodness your trolley isn't heading north east, right? But then . . . you see on your CCTV that two kids have wandered on to the north track – the trolley is about ten seconds away from an irreversible collision with those two children. Unless you divert it in the next eight seconds it will kill them both. But if you divert it north east it will be you who has diverted it towards the child you spotted on the north east track. If you divert it, you are sentencing that child to death. You've got four seconds left – do you want to kill that child? Three . . . two . . . one . . . Did you divert it?

Many people find it hard to take the direct action to divert the trolley and kill the one child and most prefer to do nothing even though it will kill two children. The reason? We feel more responsible when we proactively initiate an action than when we stand back and allow an action to happen – even if that (at least rationally and objectively) seems to end up with a worse outcome. Ultimately, we don't want to take actions that cause losses and are often prepared to suffer more loss or worse outcomes so long as we perceive that our inaction (leaving the trolley to do its thing) is less casually related to an outcome than an action that we purposefully took (putting our hands on the lever that directed it to the child playing on their own).

Of course, this is an extreme version of the problem, but the point is that we are often unable to get past the status quo of just having things stay the same (even if they are bad). And the thing is, we're not wrong to feel like this. Or at least, we're not always wrong: some psychologists have argued that maintaining the status quo often makes perfect sense. For example, Anne always takes her daily walk along the same riverside path. She knows exactly when she's done 5,000 steps and can turn back, and not having to 'think' about her route means she can focus on other things or listen to music or a podcast. Plus, she likes to see the changing seasons in the same setting. Sure, varying her route might bring all sorts of discoveries and pleasures, but the status quo frees up mental energy for Anne, and that's what she values about walking. By the same token, Bill, who has only ever owned an Apple computer, wants to stick with Apple as he knows his way round their products and doesn't want to spend time negotiating a new system. Sure, other products might bring new possibilities, but that's not what he's after right now. He needs his computer to help him with his job, he knows what tasks he needs it to do, and the possibility of gain from a new system is outweighed by the advantages of not needing to spend time on technology.

There are other positives to status quo thinking. For example, we often assume that because a particular system or way of life has been honed over many years, it must be 'better'. And, sometimes, it is. Linked to this assumption is a feeling that certain practices and traditions are worthy of a kind of respect and cherishing. For example, at a wedding some couples might want to do things a certain way because it's the way their parents did it, and their parents' parents before them. In this case, keeping to the status quo is a way of honouring the positives of the past, of paying tribute to the people who went before us and who helped make our path smoother. It's about tribute and gratitude, and these are meaningful elements of our lives. But at the same time, anyone who has planned a wedding will know that we often face decisions in which we have to juggle 'what is traditionally done' with what will make us happy. This is where it becomes important for you to recognise status quo thinking —are you doing something for the sake of not doing something else (keeping only with Apple) or are you doing it because it is the best possible option for you (Apple is the best)?

Perhaps you have sometimes found yourself thinking, 'Why am I doing this?' or 'Why am I doing this this way?' As we, along with the world in general, have experienced recently, the Covid-19 pandemic has likely made us reflect on many things we do or how we do them. An obvious one is travel. When we first entered lockdown in the UK, one thought I (Laurence) had was, 'Thank God I don't have to fly to Washington DC to do that 15-minute lecture I normally have to do.' When I heard myself think this it seemed so obviously grotesque. For several years I had made a one-hour trip to the airport, hung around for two hours for the flight and then spent ten hours in the air, an hour in the cab to the hotel and two days away from family – to present for a full 15 minutes, only to then reverse this crazy journey. I find this an almost shameful confession given the carbon footprint, the dereliction of duty to my family and the insane lack of thinking that went into an automatic acceptance of my fate because it was what I always did.

It is amazing how many things we do in our daily lives simply because they are the 'status quo'. Most are fine, and indeed do not need to be changed. My wife would find it particularly strange if I decided to sleep on 'her' side of the bed, for example, and even more strange if the decision was unpredictable and regularly changed. But there are many more important decisions that we make routinely that incur serious consequences.

If you reflect now, can you jot down or think of two positive changes that you could make by changing the status quo? Would you have made these without having been forced to make them? If not, why not? In my case and with respect to travel it was because I had got into a routine, which to my shame I'd never thought about carefully enough, even though it was causing me stress, time away from family and considerable fatigue (let alone the impact on the environment). When we are busy and we do what we always do, we don't always have the time to give ourselves the space we need to think. It's tragic to admit that a global pandemic was the only thing that stopped me in my tracks on my own crazy version of the trolley problem where I was constantly hurtling forward, never stopping and never even contemplating redirecting. What's more, I should know better!

We discussed the need for 'forces' to make us move in Chapter 2, but we shouldn't always look to an external force to impose a change on us. We need a 'looking out of the window moment' to re-evaluate what matters. Ensure you give yourself some time on a semi-regular basis to evaluate things and to contemplate change. Many of you will have experienced moments where your priorities and values changes; often it is after a life-changing event, such as having a child, getting married, a near-death experience or surviving a health scare. But remember, if your values guide your decisions (as we explored in Chapter 3), if your values change, so too must some of your decisions. Otherwise you run the risk of sleepwalking into a situation in which you are doing nothing different, but slowly violating something that is really important to you. We will talk about this more in the next chapter, but space and pace are both important in making change.

Don't Fail to Try

One thing we always say when we deliver decision-making training to law enforcement and the military is to try new things – don't show us what you normally do, try the new thing we have taught you. In training scenarios, it doesn't matter if you failed to stop the insurgents, allowed the nuclear power plant to blow up, let the virus spread or flooded the town – there are no real consequences. But if you tried something new and it worked, you've a new weapon in your armoury that you never knew you had. We need to think sometimes about the consequences of re-diverting the trolley since it may lead to a better outcome or a least bad one than the direction of travel we are currently on. Trying and failing is better than never trying, never failing and always staying the same.

However, trying new things takes conscious effort and sometimes not inconsiderable risk. There are some wonderful studies of what discriminates elite from pretty good ice skaters.[2] Do you know what you see if you spend time observing what separates the elite from the very good ones when they train? The elite ones spend way more time on their asses! Why? Because they are the ones trying the more difficult tricks. If you've ever been skating you'll know that falling on your ass hurts, which is perhaps why only some athletes are prepared to tolerate that experience over and over again. It is also why so often you see people saying that adults need to adopt 'kid-like' learning frameworks and engage more in exploration. Kids, unlike adults, are less wedded to the status quo, less afraid to lose and more open to experimentation.

Like so many concepts in this book, good decision-making is about balanced thinking. Too much of one thing can lead us down rabbit holes. Too little, and we never had a chance to grapple with the decision and really work out what was best. Persistence and change are the same. Too much change and we never make any forward motion. We all know someone who changes careers too often. And while this may be fine in your twenties, when we have decades of our working life ahead of us, this is not so helpful if at 45 we are still starting new entry-level jobs, barely building a pension and not really establishing any expertise. On the other hand, we all know someone (perhaps it is even ourselves) who has reached a glass ceiling in their current role and *knows* that the only route up is to change – but they just won't make that leap.

Perhaps you have a sense of where you are right now. Are you someone who embraces change and often will change course when a new opportunity presents itself (perhaps *just because* a new opportunity presents itself – remember Jack in Chapter 6)? Or are you someone who is too rooted in the status quo, and too rooted in doing things *the way they are done*? As we've seen, it's a question of knowing your own strengths and pitfalls, so you know what in your own psyche is preventing you from achieving the change that decisions inevitably bring.

Being gritty

The idea of persistence has become one of the more popular concepts to study in psychology in recent years. One of the most successful researchers in this area is Angela Duckworth, a psychologist at the University of Pennsylvania, who has spent the past decade focusing on the personality trait 'grit'. While we have often discussed people as being 'gritty' and intuitively known that it relates to the personality traits of digging deep, continuing when the going gets tough, etc.,

Duckworth sought to define what precisely grit is. To her, grit is defined as passion and sustained persistence applied towards long-term achievement, with no particular concern for rewards or recognition along the way.[3]

Duckworth's work focused on how to measure grit and developed a scale that has now been widely used, from young school children to members of the Armed Forces. She then began to look at the effect of being gritty; how well gritty people perform under pressure, or at their job, or even in relationships. And, overall, whether grit is a good or a bad thing.

In one of her first studies, she studied cadets at the elite United States Army West Point Military Academy.[4] Duckworth gave the cadets a short grit questionnaire in the first two or three days of the summer, along with all the other psychological tests such as IQ and the Big Five personality test. Of all the variables measured, grit was the best predictor of which cadets would stick around through that first difficult summer, when, despite the rigorous admissions guidelines and selective admission procedure, 1 in 20 cadets drops out. What was more interesting was that Duckworth and her colleagues found that grit also predicted success in a national spelling bee competition and student grade point averages at an Ivy League university. In another study, grit was more influential than cognitive or physical ability when it came to making it through the tough military training (referred to as 'Beast Barracks') that West Point cadets go through.[5]

You can look at the scale that Duckworth developed here: https://angeladuckworth.com/grit-scale/ and even calculate your own 'grittiness'; if you take the test online, it will give you an exact 'grit score'. At this point you may be asking why this is relevant to you. What does being *gritty* have to do with making decisions? Decisions, after all, are not akin to a military fitness exam. Traditional thinking has it that good decisions require intelligence and cognitive ability. And while that is true, these cognitive abilities alone are not enough and often we need non-cognitive abilities, such as good sleep, proper nutrition and controlling our emotions (outlined in Chapter 3), to help us get through when the going gets tough.

This is why grit is particularly important when making least-worst decisions. Because in order to overcome fear, and doubt, and uncertainty, and all the pressures that face you in the real world, you have to have the ability to overcome any negative feedback that you might receive. Let us think about the case of Claudia, who's a British doctor. She has worked hard over the last few years to develop a speciality in acute prenatal cardiology and, in order to become a consultant in this area, she is now required to take a position overseas. In this sense the only thing that stands between Claudia and her dream of being a consultant is to work for a spell in Canada, the best place to hone her skills. Having already spent long days and nights studying, having already taken endless exams and attended interviews, she must now let out her home in the UK and move her two children abroad. Many would understand why Claudia might, at any point in this process, have thrown her hands up in the air and declared 'enough'. But she hasn't. She has grit.

And it's grit that allows us to move past the discomfort that we feel, and even the negative feedback, to allow us to stay committed to our decision long enough to reap its rewards.

Think now about a decision you have made: perhaps a commitment to lose weight, or to take up a new sport, or to take a part-time degree to boost your qualifications. One in which you really took a chance and seized an opportunity. Was it easy? Was it plain sailing throughout? Did you know you were right from the get-go and never had a doubt in your mind about what you were doing? The likely answer to this is no. Most decisions, at least those that really matter, will be hard. There will be moments early on where you doubt yourself and you could abandon your course of action, return to the status quo, give up and do what you think is easiest. But that is where grit comes in. Decision making with known outcomes and 'right' and 'wrong' answers is cognitive. You calculate the best, or the worst, outcomes and you make your choice. Least-worst decision-making, the kind of decision-making where you have to follow your heart as much as your head, often requires grit and determination, and the ability to believe that what you are doing is right.

Do you think Tyler had doubts when he was sleeping in his car waiting for his non-profit to take off? Probably.

Do you think Michael Jordan had doubts when he was cut by his high-school basketball team? Maybe

But it didn't matter. Because even if they had doubts, they persevered. And today, we know them for their success.

In many cases, the rewards of making a decision are not instant; we don't immediately reap the benefits, we're not showered with praise, we don't taste on-the-spot happiness. Instead, we have to suffer, to persist, with grit in our heart, and bear it out. Only then can we come out the other side happier and healthier. So it's not merely making the decision that matters, we must also he committed not to abandon our course of action if and when things don't go our way.

Avoiding sunk costs

There is, however, one caveat to this – and it's something we've come back to time and again throughout this book. Grit, yes; persistence, yes: but we also need to know when enough is enough and it's time to change course.

We all know people who just won't quit, who will follow a doomed idea all the way to the very end because they are convinced that if they *just invest more* everything will be OK. It's a trap, and human beings often fall into it. When I (Neil) was 18, I did a ski season and lived in the mountains of Switzerland, serving breakfast to hotel guests in the morning, snowboarding all afternoon and then being back in time to serve dinner. It was a corporate business structure in which the company recruited as many young individuals as possible, gave them a roof, food, a ski pass and as little money as they legally could and, in return, we worked full-time at the ski resort hotels. On the inside it was an interesting micro-culture of what we called 'seasonaires' – those who were there for the season, rather than just a week's holiday (which formed some sort of organic resort hierarchy between seasonaires and everyone else). By the third month of the season the bosses would come around and ask 'Where do you want to go next season?' and the workers could pick a country and a resort and sign away another winter of their lives. I remember the strange look I got when I said that I was only doing one season because I had to go to university. I remember seeing all these people who, despite living an incredible life of snowboarding and constant travelling, were trapped in this micro-world of never-changing or breaking the seasonaire cycle. One friend of mine, who had done six seasons when I did mine, told me he hated doing them, but was continuing because he 'just wanted to do ten'.

This is another way that we can often find ourselves resistant to change, not because of the fear of doing something new, but because of the fear of losing what we have. It's called the 'sunk cost principle' and it goes like this: if we've invested in something, we naturally want to stick with it because we're wired to want to make something come good once we've put effort, time or money, or even all three, into it. Now as you read that you're quite probably thinking 'of course', because it's a pretty core instinct for most of us. And often, it's a very useful one: it inspires us to stick with the daily difficult realities of family life, for example, because we recognise that important things like creating strong bonds with our partner or children involve, very often, just keeping on going even when we'd much rather give up.

But consider this: the sunk cost principle can work against us too, because it steers us towards allowing our past choices to influence our future ones – and in doing so, it militates against the rejuvenation and reassessment that keeps life feeling fresh. Where it bites is at the point where it's pushing you to stick with a situation that's making you unhappy or worse off; and making matters potentially worse is the fact that the more you've invested or sunk into making your relationship, your career choice or your living situation work, the more you'll be loath to discard all that input, even though part of you knows there are alternatives that could bring a happier, more fulfilled, more successful life. Once again, it's loss that shouts loudest in our brains: what about all that time you spent at college, and then the long years when you were trying to establish yourself; or the time you spent with your partner trying to improve your relationship, not to mention the time and money you invested in couples counselling?

Here's an example from a university setting that shows how pervasive sunk costs can be, and how easily we can find ourselves trapped by the investments we have already made. It centres on Destiny, who studied business at a leading UK university and graduated with top honours. Not unsurprisingly, she then found herself getting accepted on to the graduate scheme at a top London business firm, and was eventually leading a team of 15 and running a multi-million-dollar portfolio.

This all sounds good, right? The problem is, Destiny never really liked business – but the further she advanced, the harder it was to do anything else. She had, after all, invested so much. In her first year at university, she was told that to change her degree subject she would have to abandon an entire year (and pay another year of fees). After graduation she couldn't go back and do another degree immediately, and ten years later she was doing so well she couldn't abandon her job and start all over again.

The more successful she became, the harder it was for her to abandon her path.

But these sunk costs started building from the minute she went to university. It is interesting to note that in the United States there is a far more lenient policy at college that means students can attend 'undeclared' and are not subject to the same pressures. They can almost change major at any time if they want to, though this can lead to the opposite issue in which people can be at college for years without knowing what major they even want to graduate with! Like everything, it is about balance: we need to value our investment so we do not abandon things that matter, but we cannot be so trapped by it that we cannot change our path when we are unhappy.

When we invest time in something we do so with the expectation that we'll stick with it, so pulling the plug feels like failure. Unsurprisingly, research has discovered a direct correlation between the amount of investment and how keen we are to cling on. In one US study, psychologists asked people to imagine they'd accidentally double-booked two trips away for the same weekend.[6] One was to Montreal, the other to Cancun. They'd have to choose and when told there was a big price difference – one flight had cost USD$200, the other USD$800 – people overwhelmingly opted for the more expensive trip, even if they preferred the idea of the cheaper destination.

Strangely it's not just our own personal investment that speaks to us: we're willing to change our behaviour (or stick with the status quo) to reflect someone else's investment, too. Here is another example. Imagine you are at a dinner event that you've had to pay for ahead of time. You get to the party and the host asks whether you'd like some cake. Though it looks really fancy, you're just not hungry and so you decline. But then your partner reminds you, 'The dinner party cost a fortune. We never do this – go on, treat yourself!' Often, what may compel us to indulge is simply being reminded of what this piece of cake we are about to decline has cost someone.

So human investment – certainly our own, but even other people's – is something we feel a very strong obligation not to ignore. And that means there's yet another inbuilt stalling device that tries to hold us back from the change that goes hand in hand with effective decision-making.

Knowing when to keep going

At this point your head may be swimming and you may be thinking that this entire chapter has been a verbal circle in which we have talked you into persisting when the going gets tough, but then changing the status quo and abandoning courses of action because change is good for you. The question you are now likely screaming at the book is 'WHICH ONE DO I DO?' How do you know whether you should persist or not? Better yet, when do you persist and when do you stop sinking costs into a lost cause (without really knowing if the cause is lost or not)?

To answer this question, you need to know two things:

1. What is your reason for persisting (or indeed your reason to no longer persist)?

2. Is the goal you are currently striving for one that is truly important to you?

The idea of knowing why you are persisting is a really important one – and indeed it's the sole divider between 'grit' and 'banging your head against a wall again and again, even when your head is bleeding'. The former is a much-needed personal ability to get through tough times; the latter is the bull-headed refusal to give up on a task without any positive gain. It is a fine line and one that even theoretically people have struggled to think about. How do we even measure that moment in which persistence becomes a problem?

Recently a colleague of ours, Matthew Crayne, wanted to capture this idea of persistence as a double-edged sword. He and his colleague Matthew Howard (a researcher at the University of South Alabama) agreed that some forms of persistence (such as grit) are good, they keep people going when the going gets tough and, as we saw with Duckworth's work, they predict success.[7] But other forms of persistence are not so helpful – instead they may be the types of persistence that manifest in trying to make a failed relationship work for ten years or staying too long in a job. They proposed that persistence is made up of three different subsets of factors:

1. persistence despite difficulty

2. persistence despite fear

3. inappropriate persistence

Below we outline some of the questions used within each scale so you can see that, while all involve persistence, all three are actually quite different. Again, when you read/ hear each statement, think to yourself how much you agree with it – does it describe you?

Persistence despite difficulty:

- I keep on going when the going gets tough.
- People describe me as someone who can stick at a task, even when it gets difficult.
- Even if it's difficult to understand, I will read an entire book until I 'get' it.

Persistence despite fear:

- I tend to face my fears.
- Even if I feel terrified, I will stay in that situation until I have done what I need to do.
- I stay persistent even when I am scared of things.

Inappropriate persistence:

- Sometimes I find myself continuing to do something, even when there is no point in carrying on.
- Sometimes I will keep doing the same thing over and over, but I believe that it is normal to do so.
- I will keep trying at something, even if I know my actions are worthless.

As you went through those questions, which did you find yourself agreeing with? Was it the first three questions – the ones that relate to your ability to overcome adversity and difficulty and keep going? If the answer is yes, you clearly persist when the going gets tough. When you are presented with a difficult challenge or situation, you do not shy away from the fact it is 'hard' and not straightforward, and you embrace the challenge. If that did not describe you, perhaps you are too quick to abandon things when you hid a roadblock or face your first hurdle.

What about the second set of questions; do these describe you? If so, then you have the ability to persist despite being scared.

Perhaps you are getting even more of a sense about yourself and your tendencies, because now we are not only tapping into *if* you persist, but *why* you persist, and why you may not. Are you likely to quit or not make the hard choice if you are scared or if it is difficult? Perhaps it is both? As with all things, knowing your 'triggers' and what makes you less likely to face a challenge is the only way you can face up to them.

This then brings us on to the third, and indeed most interesting, form of persistence – inappropriate persistence; the idea that you persist even when you are gaining nothing from it. How did you find yourself answering these questions? Did you mostly agree to them? If so, this means that you have a tendency to continue onwards for the sake of continuing onwards. Inappropriate persistence has many forms: we can try to stay friends with an ex-partner, just because we think we should (even though it causes us no happiness); we can continue to take apart a shower without calling a far more capable relative (because we think we can fix it if we just keep removing screws); in a business world, this may look like persisting on a doomed project, costing the company time and money on something you know is not going to work; or in a political world, this may look like sending more and more troops into an unwinnable war. Look around you. How many people, companies, and even countries are persisting for the sake of persisting? It is a cycle we all need to know how to break. This is inappropriate persistence; you are guided by the want to persist and not by what this persistence is meant to get you in the long run.

To Change or Not to Change?

Real change is often precisely what we need to live better lives, and there are many examples of people who have somehow managed to keep their foot on the gas and to engineer a whole new direction. For a famous example, look at the Harry Potter creator J. K. Rowling: she was a single parent with a young child, living mostly on benefits, when she had an idea while on a train from Manchester to London.[8]

At the time, Rowling was feeling a failure. It must have been tempting to find a new job as a researcher or secretary (jobs she had done before) and to simply carry on. But her idea for a boy wizard, who would travel on a magical train journey across Scotland as well as enjoying all sorts of other adventures, had taken root in her heart, and she decided to focus everything on writing her novel and finding a publisher for it (though in relation to our discussion on persistence before, it is worth mentioning that her book was rejected by 12 publishers before it was finally published). Today the Harry Potter series has sold more than 500 million copies, making it the top bestselling book series in history. Rowling is a billionaire author – the world's first, according to Forbes.

By daring to change, she found a future that was incomparable to her past. She found the strength to override the voices that must have urged her to stay safe, to choose the status quo over change – and as well as her life being utterly transformed, she also gave the world's children the gift of one of the best-loved fictional characters in human history.

Or there's Ricky Gervais, who spent his twenties attempting to make it in pop music, working first as the singer of a new-wave band called Seona Dancing, and then as manager of the band Suede.[9] It wasn't until he was in his thirties that the idea of writing comedy came his way after he met the person who became his co-writer, Stephen Merchant. If he'd stuck with music, we'd never have had *The Office*, *After*

Life – or any of his Golden Globe award appearances. Like Rowling, Gervais overcame inertia and opted for change.

Clearly, then, we do have the ability to change – so what makes the difference? As we've argued, part of what you need is just to know this stuff because then you can second-guess your brain. While your instinct might be for the same, your life might be better served by taking the decision to make the change that feels uncomfortable and unpalatable.

Be guided by the right principles

Now that you know that change, and specifically the idea of knowing when to change what you are currently doing, is not only difficult, but fraught with psychological traps that are waiting to trick you into avoiding that much-needed change, or continuing down the current path you are on despite getting nothing from it, what can help you override that instinct for the status quo? Well, it's something we've already discussed: it all comes down to knowing what your sacred values are and tapping into them (see page 81).

Your sacred values – the principles and rules that you adhere to in the deepest part of yourself – are your guide to when change is right for you. Knowing those values will give you the strength to counter the instinct to stick with the 'same old'. In essence, it's all about working out what truly, absolutely matters to you – and then daring to go through with the actions that will put them at the very centre of your life.

With all this in mind, let's visit an example that shows how our values can help us navigate this minefield of persistence. We want you to imagine that you and two friends are climbing a mountain. For the purpose of the exercise, let's call your friends Luke and Chris. All of you are in your late teens and none of you are hugely experienced climbers. You have a decent knowledge of the mountain range since you live locally, but none of you have hiked in the weather you now find yourselves in.

As you near the top of the north ridge of the mountain, the weather changes dramatically. Having been a bright and sunny day, in the last 30 minutes it turns to sheeting rain and high winds. Suddenly, Chris exclaims, 'I don't want to go to the top . . . This is freaking me out. I think we need to go immediately back down.'

Luke responds with, 'No way – you go down if you have to, but we are less than five minutes from the top. I'm going up.'

Luke then begins to ascend, and you think, 'What are we going to do?' There is no obvious leader, but decisions need to be made. Given that Luke has decided he doesn't mind abandoning one of your group, and Chris by his own admission is freaking out, what happens next comes down to you. What are you going to do – knowing that, realistically, who you side with will likely be the decision that the entire group sticks with?

Let's look to our trolley problem as a framework and, in doing so, we are going to consider not human beings on the line, but value systems. Think about which ones you are prepared to run over and which you are prepared to save.

Take a moment to draw out your trolley tracks: draw a single line to represent 'north'. What will you lose if you go with Chris? Now draw on the line all the things that this current direction of travel is running over – it might be your pride, your own sense of achievement, your want to be the best at everything you do and to fulfil promises you made. It might also be the fact that you have to abandon the last eight hours of climbing just 30 minutes before the summit. You also have your friendship to Luke, who may (or may not) handle your decision well. Be as concrete as you can about what you are running over.

Now draw another track that provides you with an alternative route in which you are not sacrificing all these things, but are running over a host of new values associated with following Luke. These would include the fact you are placing your friends at risk, you are sacrificing your relationship with Chris who is clearly upset and you are prioritising immaterial things over large-scale material concerns, like getting home safely and seeing your family.

As you look at what you've jotted down, think about your values: remember what they are – especially the sacred ones. Name them: say them out loud. And then looking at the trolley tracks you've drawn, ask yourself: what values am I serving by continuing down those lines I'm already on? Are they serving my values or have I somehow got caught up in the values of another person or another organisation? Have you adopted Luke's value of bull-headed commitment over your own? Or have you allowed Chris's temporary meltdown to make you question how very close you are to the top of the mountain? If so, you need to redirect yourself on to a path where what you're serving is your own values, because the last thing you want in life is to be investing a great deal of time and energy in a path that doesn't reflect who you truly are. This is true if you decide to go back down the mountain or take those last few difficult steps to the top.

We will close this chapter with one last tale of persistence despite difficulty. A few years ago, I (Neil) took part in a charity event that involved 'yomping' (a mix of hiking/ jogging) 30 miles with 30kg on my back. It meant driving the length of the country, checking in to a small bed and breakfast in the middle of nowhere, attending a 'pre-event safety briefing', grabbing five hours' sleep and then getting ready to do 30 miles of hell the next day. I knew no one at the event; everyone who had 'committed' had since backed out. My training had been interrupted by a family cruise and, to be honest, I was spending two days driving north at the cost of seeing my own family.

I remember clearly the night before the event. I had barely eaten a carb all day and I seriously wondered if I should just go home. But I didn't, as daunting as it was. In the end, of the 30 people who set off, only nine finished – including me. To this day I look back at that event and maintain that it is the proudest achievement of my life, precisely because of the many reasons I had to quit. But the reason I didn't was that I knew deep down what my driving values were. Not giving up was sacred to me and, at every moment during that event – from deciding to do it, to planning it, to actually running it – I could have redirected the trolley and run over my sacred value. Yes, that would have been easier. Yes, I could have rationalised it. But I know that I would have come home ashamed at myself for running over values that I hold as sacred. In your life, when you think of the decisions that you are most proud of, ask yourself: how easy was it to redirect the trolley? Or perhaps when you think of the decisions you regret the most, did you redirect the trolley too soon?

This is why values matter so much. It is not just that they help us decide what to do, but they help us know when to embrace the difficult path and persist. And even though we cannot guarantee that we will achieve our dreams, it is the knowledge that we are persisting in support of what truly matters to us that is critical to ensuring we know when to embrace the difficult path and, critically, when to abandon it.

DECISION TIME TIPS

1. Know your why! Why are you persisting? How do you know if you are working away at a dead end or just about to break through that last barrier and enjoy all the benefits of your course of action? The fact is we cannot always know the answers, but what we can know is if we are persisting (or not) for the right reasons. Next time the going gets tough, ask yourself:

   - Do I want to give up because I am scared?
   - Do I want to give up because it is difficult?

2. Desirable difficulties are a good thing! Avoiding hardship will not lead to happiness. Hardship makes you stronger – especially if it is in the pursuit of something that is in line with your values.

---

3. If you are persisting and you aren't getting the results you are hoping for, are you persisting just for the sake of not giving up? Sometimes you need to know when you need to let go of an idea, a career or a plan, even if you have invested a lot in it.

4. Keep your values at the centre of your life: identify them, think about them often and, when you make choices because of them, remind yourself why you're doing that. Be very honest with yourself about your values and whether you're truly serving them or simply paying lip service to them. It doesn't matter what it looks like: it's how you feel inside about what matters to you and whether you're truly living by those principles.

CHAPTER 8

Resilience and Recovery

Takes a lickin' but keeps on tickin'.

THAT WAS THE slogan on the Timex adverts in the fifties and sixties, and it was all about the resilience of the company's watches. To prove their point, Timex put their product into a washing machine. They tied it to an outboard motor. They hung it on a wall and fired an arrow at it. And every single time, the watch survived. It went on tickin'.[1]

The good news is that not only can we human beings go on tickin' in the face of adversity, we can go one better. While a Timex watch can survive the onslaught of being run through a wash cycle, dragged through a river or hit by an arrow, it won't actually be improved by it. But for us, that's a genuine possibility. Happily, resilience is a quality we all possess – and, if we know and believe that, we can learn strategies that enable us to not only survive, but to thrive on life beyond a crossroads moment, even if it was totally unexpected or completely seismic.

What Is Resilience?

We'd define resilience as an organism's ability to adapt in the face of disequilibrium. The more resilient the organism, the more able it is to adapt to the intensity, duration, repetition, variation and chronicity of the disequilibrium.

Another definition that's been suggested is that resilience is an individual's ability to bend but not break; to bounce back, and perhaps even to grow and become stronger in the face of adverse life experiences.

And here's a third way of defining it, perhaps even more positively: resilience is a process to harness resources to sustain well-being. This definition gives resilience an active role in improving our lives.

Over the last few years, more and more psychological research has focused on resilience. After a period in which the spotlight was on trauma and people's response to it, the study of resilience has emerged as one of the most beneficial and hopeful strands of scientific research. Those scientists who were studying trauma, and PTSD in particular, noticed something surprising about people who had experienced it. Often, they had managed to fold even incredibly difficult life events into their being in a way that made them more balanced, secure and even happy individuals. They'd never have chosen the trauma, of course. But trauma isn't something any of us choose; it's something that happens, and the focus here is on what we do when it happens, as it inevitably will. And the reason we're ending this book by putting resilience centre stage is that we know, because you've picked the book off the shelf, that you're facing, or you're anticipating, a complicated, emotional, major life decision. Perhaps you're at a crossroads you engineered; or maybe you're in a place you'd never have imagined you'd find yourself. Either way, trauma is involved; and either way, resilience is the key to what happens next.

Warning Signs

At the start of the Covid-19 pandemic in 2020 and at our own instigation we worked together as a team (alongside some academic and military colleagues) to roll out a set of resources under the banner of what became known as 'Project ARES' (Adaptive Responses for Emergency Responses). We even managed to get some celebrities and public spotlight military to help advertise it (including James Blunt, Myleene Klass, Fay Ripley, Imogen Stubbs, Ollie Ollerton and Jason Fox). It was aimed at boosting the resilience of the thousands of NHS staff working in incredibly difficult circumstances. We were well aware from our research that many of these individuals would be at high risk of depression and burnout, given what they were up against and the extraordinarily tough circumstances they faced. We knew, for example, that as many as one in four of the responders to Hurricane Katrina suffered serious mental health fallout afterwards. This was linked with not only the pressures of what they were facing in their work, but also the fact that as well as helping others to deal with the aftermath of the disaster, they were also themselves personally affected by it. And we knew that the pandemic brought the same set of circumstances: nurses, doctors, care assistants and NHS managers were also family members with relatives who were vulnerable to Covid-19, and their lives were being limited, and hence made more stressful, by the restrictions the UK government, like so many other governments around the world, introduced.

We knew, too, that the right messages on resilience could make an enormous difference. We knew that if we could arm NHS workers with information about what to expect in the months ahead, and if we offered them strategies to deal with the fallout from the Covid onslaught, we could help prevent PTSD and mental health problems going forward. We'd like to share with you some of the themes and messages of Project ARES, because while they were a response to a period of national trauma, we feel they have much to offer individuals going through personal trauma as well. And note, what we provided was not deep counselling approaches (important though these may be, especially in the aftermath); it was a set of resources to enhance resilience during the incident and help inoculate people against longer-term impacts.

One of the reasons we knew that resilience was going to be so important was the decisions that medical professionals in the NHS were being faced with. The British Medical Association (BMA), the union for doctors in the UK, even outlined that in certain conditions it would be lawful and ethical for a doctor, following appropriate prioritisation policies, to refuse someone potentially life-saving treatment where someone else has a higher priority for it. The BMA noted that doctors would face grave decisions which would require them to re-think their own moral intuitions.[2] Can you imagine spending your life dedicated to saving lives, to then be placed in a situation where the *most* ethical decision may be to not give a patient treatment? These were the kind of decisions that the Covid-19 pandemic was forcing upon healthcare workers, and why we knew that resilience was going to be one of the most important skills. We couldn't remove the need to make these awful decisions, but we could help the NHS be resilient to the immense strain these decisions placed on them.

As a starting point we took the work we'd done with the military and law enforcement agencies, because we believed we would be able to adapt lessons learned for the NHS staff, for whom such tough working conditions and pressurised decision-making was less practised. We focused our initial work on what we call the 'Prepare' and 'Adapt' phases of dealing with a critical situation. The 'Prepare' phase gets people ready for what they're about to face: we could call it 'psychological PPE'. Being aware of what's going on inside your head and within your body, both during the run-up to a stressful situation and then during the stressful situation itself, makes bearing it a great deal easier when it actually takes place, and it makes it easier to move on from it afterwards. The 'Adapt' phase involves responding as effectively as possible on a daily basis and learning to harness what is working and drop what is not.

Here's what we know: a stressful situation causes both physical and emotional symptoms, and these can lead to behavioural changes. Being aware of these symptoms and alert for the behavioural changes allows you to intervene, and if necessary seek help, before you're depressed or burned out.

Let's look at these symptoms and behavioural changes in turn.

Physical symptoms: These are often the first effects you'll feel because, as we've already explained, your body is wired to react physically to stress. We're talking about symptoms such as:

- fatigue: feeling tired the whole time
- sleep difficulties: not being able to fall asleep, waking up and not being able to get back to sleep, night-time sweats, nightmares
- headaches
- gastrointestinal issues
- colds and flu: if you're run down, you're more prone to infection

Emotional symptoms: Our physical and emotional states are so closely connected that it's hard to separate them. Stress will affect you emotionally just as it does physically – and physical symptoms will also impact on your mental health in a vicious circle, making things even worse. Emotional symptoms of stress include:

- irritability
- anxiety
- depression

- pessimism
- defensiveness
- depersonalisation
- a loss of joy
- a loss of connection to those around you
- a low sense of personal accomplishment
- a 'need' for alcohol or drugs to help you cope

Behavioural changes: The fallout from these strains on your mind and body can cause changes to your own behaviour; sometimes quickly, sometimes more gradually. We're talking about, for example:

- poor work performance
- substance abuse
- withdrawal and isolation from others
- depressed libido

Build your support network

We know people facing stressful situations are at risk of all these changes, but we also know that there are many things they can be aware of from the outset, which help boost their resilience and give them the best chance of avoiding problems.

One of the most effective ways of increasing your resilience ahead of a stressful event – or in anticipation of a stressful event that will one day come your way – is to bolster your support network. This may be easier said than done: some people find it easier to connect with family and friends than others, and life circumstances may already have conspired to deplete your support system. However, we would argue that, even if you find social interaction difficult, and perhaps especially if you find it difficult, having connections with others is the surest way of helping you survive tough times. This doesn't mean that you have to join some touchy-feely support network or that you have to sign up to every group in sight. But reaching out even a bit goes a long way: talk to neighbours; phone a friend you've not seen for a while; plan a trip that will give you an excuse to see some relatives. Connecting with other people is one of the best ways we have of keeping ourselves mentally healthy.

If you live in a nuclear family, these people are – potentially at least – far and away the cornerstone of your support system. And your relationship with your partner and/or children isn't something to neglect and ignore, no matter how busy you are in the rest of your life. In the eye of the storm, looking after your family relationships becomes far more, not less, important – the time you invest there will more than repay itself in terms of how much you have to give to the rest of your life and, most importantly, you'll be happier and you'll be healthier.

The Four Pillars of Resilience

Whatever major decision or life crisis you're facing, working on your resilience is the best tool you have to not only make it through, but make it through with – as we've emphasised throughout this book – a better deal for yourself on the other side. Happily, the world isn't divided into people who are resilient and people who aren't. A whole raft of research backs up what evolution suggests, which is that human beings have the potential for resilience written into their DNA.[3] All of us can survive when we're up against it, and there's a way of approaching life that can help.

We call it 'the four pillars of resilience', and we describe them in detail below. The key is not to obsess about them, but rather to ensure that you don't ignore any of the areas that contribute to making you more resilient. If you're under particular strain, you shouldn't be surprised if some pillars weaken: in the same way that you can't maintain all the parts of your house to perfection at all times, so you can't continually have four perfect resilience pillars. But just as you don't want to allow the plumbing, brickwork, gas and electric wiring to degrade, for the maintenance of your resilience you need to work on all four of these areas.

Health

Being put in positions where we have to (or will have to) make a hard decision taxes the body as much as it taxes the mind. So, to be resilient to these kinds of stressful situations, we need to make sure that we are taking care of our health. How many times have you tried improving your diet and exercise regime, only to revert to fast food and a sedentary lifestyle? The truth is, though, that long-term change really can help and really is important. The secret is to start small:

making small changes to your lifestyle means you're more likely to keep them going. Set yourself a realistic step target for your walking each day, and eventually you can move towards increasing it, or adding in different exercise as well. Stop buying cakes and biscuits in your weekly shop, but once in a while allow yourself to make a special trip to buy a treat. Remember that your healthy diet starts in the supermarket: if it's not in your house, it's a lot less likely to end up in your body. In addition, one of the things we see with military personnel is an unwavering regular commitment to exercise. This is such a habit that even if in a bunker and in a confined space military personnel will find some way to be active on a regular and predictable basis. For the rest of us, this doesn't mean paying for gym membership, buying expensive exercise equipment or spending time trying to best yourself. But it does mean predictable, regimented effort. Not all the time but MOST of the time. A run, a walk, some press-ups . . . it doesn't matter which. What matters is doing some physical exercise on a semi-regular basis – especially if, like us, you have a sedentary job.

Purpose

Earlier in this book we discussed the importance of knowing your values and making decisions in line with those values. This does not just help you make decisions, it helps you be resilient throughout these situations because it gives you a clear sense of what your purpose is. We need to feel life is meaningful. If you feel that much of your day,

day after day, is taken up with pointless and thankless tasks, that is a real problem. We all accept some boring tasks that we have to do, but we also need to imbue life with purpose. In a crisis, our sense of agency feels as though it's being eroded (this is normal), but we can't maintain that mindset: we have to fight back, even if only in a tiny way. Finding meaning in your work is a very effective way to have purpose in your life, since we spend so much of our lives working, but there are other ways to find meaning, through hobbies and voluntary work. In fact, helping others is one of the best ways to tick the purpose box. You don't have to throw yourself into the fire, but a small step forward will help others and in doing so help you.

Joy

The process of making hard decisions may not be fun, but we cannot let the stress of making decisions hold us back from the joy that enacting a decision can bring. Do not be so focused on what you had to sacrifice that you fail to maximise what you set out to gain. Feeling the joy of decisions is critical to resilience. This is the fun pillar, but often it's also the most neglected. In some ways it's the opposite of being purposeful. It's laughing, dancing, drawing, sharing food with friends; as military folks say, it's about finding cheerfulness in the face of adversity. Again, you don't need to worry if you don't feel joy every day of your life – it's OK to weep, to be sad, to be disorganised (and then to feel guilty), and sometimes you're just not in the mood for fun. But if avoiding the fun things in life becomes a long-term pattern, that's a very real problem. Often the best soldiers are the ones who keep morale high by being either the joker or the butt of the jokes of others. And remember, joy doesn't have to be virtuous: in fact, the sillier, more juvenile and frivolous the fun, the better it often is.

Feedback

Sometimes when making decisions, we make multiple sequential decisions in order to navigate a situation. Other times, we make large decisions years apart. In either case, do not forget to reflect on how you made these past decisions, what you learned about yourself and what you did well (or not so well). In our working lives, lateral (across teams) and vertical (chain of command) feedback is critical, both good and bad. Resilience means being able to adapt, and where something works it needs to be shared; by the same token, problems (both logistic and emotional) also need to be communicated. On long-term military deployments soldiers often end up finding themselves without adequate provisions, kit and information. They need to pass that up the line and, critically, senior officers have to indicate that they have heard it, even if they can't solve it. From a leadership perspective, emotional intelligence is every bit as critical as rational intelligence; and in our individual lives too, acknowledging in ourselves and to others how we're feeling can be the difference between the ability to thrive, as opposed to managing to just about survive.

The lessons of failure

Someone in my (Laurence's) life who understood very well the importance of emotional intelligence was Professor Aidan Halligan, a surgeon who worked creatively for many years to create safer and more effective healthcare, in roles including deputy chief medical officer for England and director of clinical governance for the NHS.

One of his key messages, and it's one we endorse absolutely, was that failure is key to creating resilience – so although it's natural to want to avoid failure, it's also very useful to understand its potential in our lives. Failure, Aidan believed, has an almost unrivalled role, in that it gives us opportunities for growth that allow us to bounce back from difficulties and recover. What we can't do, he said, is avoid making mistakes: that's a given. If you're a human being and you're alive, mistakes are something you'll make.

Failure is one of life's most potent teachers, but many of us reduce its power in our lives. Instead of welcoming the chance to learn from a mistake, we beat ourselves up about what's happened; we blame ourselves, we allow guilt to wear us down, we're self-critical and we look inwards rather than outwards. While a measure of self-blame and guilt is, of course, absolutely natural – no one likes to screw up, and guilt is a necessary human emotion – if negativity becomes stifling, if our failure becomes something we obsess over, we lose the huge opportunities it also offers. Resilience means being kind to yourself; showing yourself compassion. Everyone makes mistakes: it's what happens next that matters.

The Good Habits of Resilient People

Another exceptionally impressive thinker on resilience is Lucy Hone. In 2014 she was an academic researching resilience and its place in life, when an appalling tragedy took the life of her 12-year-old daughter in a car crash. As she says, the loss of a child for a parent is probably the toughest trauma there is in human life: if there was ever a loss an individual felt they were never going to recover from, it would be this one. But Lucy already knew that resilience is a power every human being can harness; she already knew the tools that would help her get through this hardest of experiences and she was determined to make them work. In a TED Talk in 2019 she explained the habits that resilient people share that make all the difference:[4]

- Resilient people know that bad things happen.
  Resilient people understand in their hearts that suffering is part of life; so, when they're up against it, when they find themselves in a traumatic situation, they don't think 'Why me?' and they don't imagine that life is somehow ranged against them. They know this isn't bad luck or think that life has got it in for them; instead, they know that what they're going through is part and parcel of being alive. No one has a perfect life; no one has an existence that isn't laced with difficult times. If you can accept that life will bring difficulties, and sometimes these will be major ones, you will already be one step ahead in making it through them.

- Resilient people are good at choosing where to direct their attention. They're good at putting what's sometimes called the 'Serenity Prayer' into practice:[5]

    Give me the serenity to accept the things I cannot change,
    courage to change the things I can,
    and wisdom to know the difference.

    Understanding the difference between what we can and cannot change is a crucial skill for resilience; it allows us to spend our emotional energy where it can be most effective, rather than using it up in areas of our lives where it either makes no difference to our mental health or even undermines it. In essence, it's about not losing what you've still got to what you've already lost; it's about counting your blessings, even in the toughest of times (and that's what Lucy did, focusing on her two other children, her sons, who, as she said, deserved to have a happy home life despite the loss of their sister).

- Resilient people ask themselves: 'Is what I'm doing helping me or harming me?' In other words, they're kind to themselves; they deliberately disconnect from thoughts or behaviours that undermine their mental health. People who've gone through a relationship break-up often torment themselves by obsessively following their ex on social media: if that's you, ask yourself whether you're helping or harming yourself. And if the thoughts or behaviour you're engaging in seem too big to just move on from, give yourself 'breaks' from them: have an hour when you don't scroll through your ex's social media, and then build up to a whole day.

Resilience is what gets us through the storms in which we make the most difficult decisions of our lives; and it's also what gives us the energy to keep on going along the path we've decided to take, even when the going gets tough. What's more, believing in our own resilience prepares us for the inevitable future maelstroms we will experience – it's a self-replenishing element of our psyche, in that surviving one trauma, making decisions and moving on from it arms you for the next by giving you confidence. Next time you're at a crossroads and having to make a major life choice, you'll be able to think back to last time. You survived then, and you'll survive now.

DECISION TIME TIPS

1. Trauma cannot be avoided, so accept that what you are going to do may be hard. Accepting you need to make a decision will be hard, deciding will be hard, implementing that decision will be hard and the immediate aftermath (and long-term effects) could be hard too. But not deciding, or avoiding, because of a fear of taking the 'tough path', while easier in the short run, could lead to more unhappiness in the long

run. As Lucy Hone says in her TED Talk, if we can accept that life will bring difficulties, sometimes major ones, we will already be a step ahead when it comes to making it through them.'[6]

2. Be in tune with yourself and how you are feeling: monitor your sleep, your diet and how your body is feeling.

3. Trust your friends and family. Too often we suffer in silence. Share your decisions, if you can. In the army they call this an 'after action review' and part of it is cathartic. Debrief with loved ones.

4. Believe in your own capacity for resilience. We are programmed to bounce back. We will recover.

Time to Face Your Decisions

'M HOPELESS AT making decisions', 'I worry I'll go down a path I'll come to regret', 'I'm haunted by the "what ifs" of how things might have been.' We've all heard people voicing fears like these; perhaps you used to be one of them yourself. If so, we hope you've reached the end of this book feeling very different and now have the confidence to believe in yourself as an effective decision maker. Of course, we all vary in how we tackle things and some of us do struggle to move forward. That said, you should now be armed with all the basics that will help you. And, if you are the sort of person who finds forward momentum less problematic, then you, too, should be able now to harness what it is you do naturally and use it to even more powerful effect.

When you're faced with a watershed moment and you know the option you take is going to affect your own and perhaps others' lives in profound ways, you might wish you could pass on the choice or that someone else could simply tell you what to do. But, as we've seen, sound decision-making is inextricably linked to your unique value system: your choices must reflect who you are and what you believe in. To do that, you need to dig deep, be honest with yourself and identify what matters to you and why. If you've not listed these things at any other point in the book, do it now. Take a moment to really think about what you value and what you believe in. Try to be as precise as possible – this is even more critical if you are considering a specific decision right now.

Knowing yourself is a prerequisite for sound decision-making. It's a skill you must hone well ahead of approaching a major crossroads. After all, if you don't know the destination, how can you begin to consider which is the best path to get there? If you spend time focusing now on your values, you'll find you'll be able to make the next major decision in your life more quickly, and more easily.

Sometimes we delude ourselves about values and think that, for example, they are connected to monetary issues, are job-related or are about possessions. However, these are usually drivers of values rather than values in themselves. Your job matters to you because working hard and achieving all that you're capable of are your underlying values. Having enough money matters because it allows you to provide for your children, and your core value is putting your family at the centre of your life. Possessions matter because they make life more fun, more enjoyable, and your core value is making the most of every moment you have in this world. So don't be hard on yourself for wanting 'things'; rather, interrogate yourself further about *why* you want these things and what they represent for you. Go deeper than the surface. Think about where the impetus for your values came from. This often helps us work out why things matter to us and also helps us separate the drivers of values from the values themselves. If you can drill down to those values, you'll be priming yourself to be the best decision maker you can possibly be.

Making major decisions is a scary part of being human, and we haven't tried in this book to shy away from how frightening or momentous they can be. In fact, it's our contention that it's precisely because a decision can be so terrifying that our instinct is often to shelve it. But that's never the answer. As we've discovered, shelving a decision is the worst thing you can do as it takes away a power that is at the core of being human – the power to discern a complex situation, to consider it from all viewpoints and to choose where to go from there to maximise events in your favour. Ignore the choice and you're giving up the chance to influence future events – and that's one of the greatest chances life offers any of us, and never one to turn down.

However, making a choice has negative as well as positive components – it involves giving things up, as well as embracing other things – and so it's understandable why we might want to shy away from making a decision. But this giving up of options is one of the biggest stalling points in decision-making because we're primed to avoid loss at all costs. It's what we most fear and it's what we most want to avoid; so however much you believe that the job you've been offered is right for you or that the person you married 20 years ago is still your soulmate, some part of you deep inside will be mourning all those other jobs you might have been doing and all those other partners you might have married. What we believe, though, is that being aware of this instinct will allow you to override it. Life offers many possibilities, but we cannot experience them all. The tragedy is when fear of what we're not going to know, where we're not going to go, who we're not going to be intimate with, stop us from tasting other experiences – when we fail to shut out all the 'maybes' and stay sitting on the fence pondering what might be instead of taking a properly calculated jump that offers us the best way forward. Of course, the flip side is that some of us race into bad decisions and give up on things too easily – and, yes, this can include relationships, jobs, and so on. So, we must also be alive to the possibility that we aren't considering other options, other means by which we can reach an ambition that fits with our value system, before we flit from one bad job or relationship to another. And, again, that comes back to our value system.

All this is the background to being an effective decision maker; it's the preparatory work, if you like, that you need to have done and to have understood. Then comes the business of how to actually make a real-life critical decision, in real time, to best effect. To do this, you need to break the decision down into four different elements and address each in turn.

These elements are our 'STAR' approach: they're at the heart of our decision-making model, and they can be applied to any situation, any crossroads, any major life conundrum. Let's look again at each component of the STAR model in turn:

1. S: 'Situational awareness' and 'storytelling'

To make an effective decision, you need to understand what's going on. You need to work out what's happened, why it's happened and what's likely to happen next. It's in the third of these requirements that the greatest judgement lies, but don't underestimate the importance of the first two scene-setters. Remember, there's no such thing as being entirely objective; a story can be told in an infinite number of ways, but it will help you best to tell it in the way that's most authentic to you. Be aware, also, about why things are happening as well as what actually is happening, and try to be open-minded about motives, vested interests, biases and prejudices. We all have these, but, as we've seen, some personality types have a greater tendency to tell a story in a less rounded way. If you recognise yourself in that description, make a conscious effort to open your mind to a broader range of possibilities, bearing in mind that if you can do that you will gain in terms of the effectiveness of your decision-making.

When it comes to the all-important forecasting – what's likely to happen next? – remember that elite decision makers hold on to neither too few possible options, nor to a huge number of possibilities. Only considering one option will narrow your vision too much. However sure you are about what's likely to happen, at least float another possibility (even if it strikes you as outlandish). We reckon you'll do best if you can hold two or three possible scenarios in your head at this stage of the decision-making process, and we suggest you include a 'best-case' scenario, a 'worst-case' scenario and an 'in between' scenario. This approach allows you to plan for the worst while hoping for the best, and allows you to set your choice against the widest possible canvas.

2. T: 'Timing'

This is a crucial foundation to effective decision-making. The first, and in many ways most fundamental, question you need to ask yourself at the outset of any decision-making process is: what time do I have? Do I have to decide this now or do I have time to think about it – and, if so, how much time do I have? Keep in mind, though, that if time is open-ended and there is no requirement to decide by a particular deadline, you may become unstuck. As we've emphasised time and again in this book, one of the biggest stumbling blocks to good decision-making is inertia: doing nothing when you should be doing something.

There are various reasons for inertia, but one of them is feeling you can postpone the decision because the external factors are bearing down on you. The fact that you have space can and should be to your advantage, but if you use it as an excuse for putting off your decision and continue to shelve it, you won't be doing yourself any favours. Instead, if your decision isn't bound by a time frame, set an artificial one for yourself and stick to it.

In the rare case that the answer to the question 'Do I need to decide now?' is 'Yes – it's urgent', we suggest you work out what we've called your 'least-worst' option; the choice where even if things don't work out well, they will work out better than the worst scenario of all.

3. A: 'Adaptation'

Time and again in our work, we've been aware of the fact that the best decision makers are often also what we call 'fluid thinkers'. That means they're open-minded and adventurous in their headspace: they're open to possibilities, and they tend to take an expansive rather than a constrained view of the world. They tend to be unafraid of exploring possibilities, even unpalatable ones. They see the world in a 360-degree way, rather than being limited to their own viewpoint or prism.

However, what we also know is that some people have a personality type that militates against their ability to be a fluid thinker. This characteristic is linked to a phenomenon called 'need for closure' (NFC) and it goes like this. Human beings are designed to seek a neat ending – it's inbuilt into our evolutionary psyche as a way of helping us cope with the uncertainty of life. But in some individuals the NFC is more pronounced, and when it comes to decision-making it can count against you. Seeking out an ending too quickly can mean you fail to clock resolutions to your situation that could have been helpful. It's a bit like running through a tunnel with a train bearing down on you and focusing so much on the light at the end that you fail to notice safety hatches alongside the track where you could shelter.

If you know you have a high NFC (see page 147 for pointers to help you work this out), then your decision-making will improve if you can train yourself to look at things more broadly and to consider a wider number of possibilities. Focus on trying to be more open to other scenarios and train yourself to consider a situation from a point of view that's different from your own.

4. R: 'Revision' and 'resilience'

Fluid thinking extends beyond NFC into an ability to revise and reassess situations into the future. This matters hugely, because the truth about life is that it's in flux the entire time. Everything changes, nothing stands still; so even the best-made decision is open to new developments that may change its durability or even its premise.

All this means that reaching a decision, and even putting it into effect, is not enough: you have to go on questioning it, revisiting it and re-examining it to ensure that it remains right for you. People sometimes get stuck in the trap of persisting even when something hasn't turned out well or is going against them. To test whether what you're feeling is despair about an impossible situation or fatigue about how demanding it is, interrogate yourself about whether you're feeling scared (and if so, what of?) or fed up with how onerous the task before you is (and if so, is that feeling justified?). It all comes back, once again, to knowing yourself and being able to tune into that instinctive voice deep inside yourself that will tell you whether you truly believe in what you're doing and why.

Being on track because you've made a sound decision doesn't diminish the need to be resilient: making a good decision doesn't cancel out, and may not even reduce, the trauma or stress of facing up to the decision in the first place. Resilience is what helps you survive the difficult situation you found yourself in and helps you carry on with the decision you know is right for you, even when the going is extremely tough. We all know the 'right' decision may very well not be the 'easy' decision, and you will need to be resilient in the face of difficulties to keep on going. In particular, you'll need to be aware of four key 'pillars': your physical health, your sense of purpose in what you're doing with your life, your sense of joy and fun and how to cultivate it and recognise its importance, and the value of feedback from others – partners, family, friends and colleagues – to assist you in going forward.

All these attributes and techniques, all these approaches and attitudes, are typical of the elite decision makers we've worked with: people who've saved lives, who've been bold, who've taken risks where they were appropriate and been prudent when it mattered. These people have hit the sweet spot on timing their actions so they don't move too quickly, or too late. They've known when to go for the best outcome, and when to settle for least-worst. They've known that challenge and dark times are a part of life, and that failures and least-worst outcomes enable us to grow. But they know, too, the importance of those moments when we have to reach for the stars, when we stretch out our arms to others, when we strive as hard as possible to be compassionate, caring, ambitious and bold.

Through our professional work, we know that these lessons can be learned. This doesn't mean that you'll succeed every time; no one, not even the most adept decision maker, manages that. But, as we've seen, failure in the short term helps you become a better decision maker in the long term, so allow yourself to make mistakes and forgive yourself when you do. Don't shy away from making decisions, because the more you make them, the better you'll become at it: and, as we've explained, the worst outcomes are often about not error, but inertia. Don't fear that you won't make the 'right' choice; be strong in the knowledge that you and only you have the ability to make the decisions that will work for you.

Being at a crossroads can be the toughest of times, the scariest of times, but it also brings the most exhilarating of times, because it offers opportunity and the possibility of change. Your life moves forward because you choose to move forward at the crossroads rather than hanging back, and that's what we hope we've encouraged you to do. We wish you all the luck with doing that. Remember what we've said: pause, think and consider – but not for too long. Be a traveller in life, not a bystander, and navigate your way successfully towards the light.

A Three-Minute Mindfulness Script

This three-minute guided meditation was produced by UCLA's Mindful Awareness Research Center (MARC). It can be accessed here: https://www.mindful.org/a-3-minute-body-scan-meditation-to-cultivate-mindfulness/ or via audio here: http://marc.ucla.edu/mpeg/Body-Scan-Meditation.mp3

1. Begin by bringing your attention into your body.

2. You can close your eyes if that's comfortable for you.

3. You can notice your body seated wherever you're seated, feeling the weight of your body on the chair, on the floor.

4. Take a few deep breaths.

5. And as you take a deep breath, bring in more oxygen, enlivening the body. And as you exhale, have a sense of relaxing more deeply.

6. You can notice your feet on the floor, notice the sensations of your feet touching the floor. The weight and pressure, vibration, heat.

7. You can notice your legs against the chair: pressure, pulsing, heaviness, lightness.

8. Notice your back against the chair.

9. Bring your attention into your stomach area. If your stomach is tense or tight, let it soften. Take a breath.

10. Notice your hands. Are your hands tense or tight? See if you can allow them to soften.

11. Notice your arms. Feel any sensation in your arms. Let your shoulders be soft.

12. Notice your neck and throat. Let them be soft. Relax.

13. Soften your jaw. Let your face and facial muscles be soft.

14. Then notice your whole body is present. Take one more breath.

15. Be aware of your whole body as best you can. Take a breath. And then when you're ready, you can open your eyes.

Endnotes

Chapter 1: Decision Time

1. Yates, J. F., Veinott, E. S., & Patalano, A. L. (2003). Hard decisions, bad decisions: On decision quality and decision aiding. In: Schneider, S. L., & Shanteau, J. C. (eds.), *Emerging Perspectives on Judgment and Decision Research.* Cambridge University Press, 13–63.
2. Klein, G., & Woods, D. D. (1993). Conclusions: Decision-making in action. In: Klein, G. A., Orasanu, J., Calderwood, R., & Zsambok, C. E. (eds.), *Decision-Making in Action: Models and Methods.* Ablex, 404–11.
3. Houghton, D. P. (2013). *The Decision Point: Six Cases in U.S. Foreign Policy Decision Making.* Oxford University Press.
4. Cohen, M. S., & Lipshitz, R. (2011). *Three Roads to Commitment: A Trimodal Theory of Decision-Making.* Haifa [unpublished work].
5. Shortland, N. D., Alison, L. J., & Moran, J. (2019). *Conflict: How Soldiers Make Impossible Decisions.* Oxford University Press.
6. Tom, S. M., Fox, C. R., Trepel, C., & Poldrack, R. A. (2007). The neural basis of loss aversion in decision-making under risk. *Science, 315*(5811), 515–8.

Chapter 2: Decision Inertia

1. Zeelenberg, M. (1999). Anticipated regret, expected feedback and behavioral decision making. *Journal of Behavioral Decision Making, 12*, 93–106.
2. Lamport, L. (1984). Buridan's principle. Technical report, SRI technical report.
3. van den Heuvel, C., Alison, L., & Crego, J. (2012). How uncertainty and accountability can derail strategic 'save life' decisions in counter-terrorism simulations: A descriptive model of choice deferral and omission bias. *Journal of Behavioral Decision Making, 25*(2), 165–87.
4. Ibid.
5. Arkes, H. R., & Ayton, P. (1999) The sunk cost and Concorde effects: Are humans less rational than lower animals? *Psychological Bulletin, 125*(5), 591–600.
6. Brehm, J. W., & Cohen, A. R. (eds.) (1962). Explorations in cognitive dissonance. Wiley.
7. Power, N., & Alison, L. (2017). Redundant deliberation about negative consequences: Decision inertia in emergency responders. *Psychology, Public Policy and Law, 23*(2), 243–58.
8. Epstein, S., & Fenz, W. D. (1965). Steepness of approach and avoidance gradients in humans as a function of experience. *Journal of Experimental Psychology, 70*(1), 1–12.
9. Reid, K. (25 Nov. 2019). 2010 Haiti earthquake: Facts, FAQs and how to help. World Vision. Retrieved from https://www.worldvision.org/disaster-relief-news-stories/2010-haiti-earthquake-facts (accessed 23 May 2021).
10. Press Association (25 Nov. 2013). Flooding cost the UK £600m in 2012. *The Guardian*. Retrieved from https://www.theguardian.com/environment/2013/nov/25/flooding-cost-uk-2012 (accessed 23 May 2021).

11. DW News (2 Nov. 2020). Merkel: 'The virus punishes half-heartedness'. Retrieved from https://www.dw.com/en/merkel-the-virus-punishes-half-heartedness/av-55478253 (accessed 23 May 2021).

Chapter 3: Know Thyself

1. Milosevic, I. (2015). *Phobias: The Psychology of Irrational Fear*. Greenwood, 196, 179.
2. Harrison, Y., & Horne, J. A. (2000). The impact of sleep deprivation on decision making: A review. *Journal of Experimental Psychology: Applied, 6*(3), 236–49.
3. Anderson, R. A., & Cui, H. (2009). Intention, action planning, and decision making in parietal-frontal circuits. *Neuron, 63*(5), 568–83.
4. Larsen, R. P. (2001). Decision-making by military students under severe stress. *Military Psychology, 13*(2), 89–98.
5. Van Deusen, M. (19 May 2020). Understanding max heart rate and why it matters for training. Whoop.com. Retrieved from https://www.whoop.com/thelocker/calculating-max-heart-rate/ (accessed 23 May 2021).
6. Shortland, N. D., McGarry, P., Thompson, L., Stevens, C., & Alison, L. J. (2021). The effect of a 3-minute mindfulness intervention, and the mediating role of maximization, on critical incident decision-making. *Frontiers in Psychology, 12*, 1942.
7. Watts, A. (2011). *The Wisdom of Insecurity: A Message for an Age of Anxiety*. Vintage.
8. Manson, M. (2016). *The Subtle Art of Not Giving a F*ck*. HarperCollins.
9. Simon, H. A. (1956). Rational choice and the structure of the environment. *Psychological Review, 63*(2), 129–38.
10. Parker, A. M., Bruine de Bruin, W., & Fischhoff, B. (2007). Maximizers versus satisficers: Decision-making styles,

competence, and outcomes. *Judgment and Decision-making*, 2(6), 342–50.

11. Shortland, N. D., Alison, L. J., & Thompson, L. (2020). Military maximizers: Examining the effect of individual differences in maximization on military decision making. *Personality and Individual Differences, 163*, 110051.

12. Manson, M. (2016). *The Subtle Art of Not Giving a F*ck.* HarperCollins.

13. Atran, S., & Axelrod, R. (2008). Reframing sacred values. *Negotiation Journal, 24*(3), 221–46; Atran, S., & Axelrod, R. (30 Jun. 2010). Why we talk to terrorists. *New York Times*; Atran, S., Axelrod, R., & Davis, R. (2007). Sacred barriers to conflict resolution. *Science, 317,* 1039–40.

14. Litz, B. T., Stein, N., Delaney, E., Lebowitz, L., Nash, W. P., Silva, C., & Maguen, S. (2009). Moral injury and moral repair in war veterans: A preliminary model and intervention strategy. *Clinical Psychology Review, 29*(8), 695–706.

15. Tetlock, P. E., Kristel, O. V., Elson, S. B., Green, M. C., & Lerner, J. S. (2000). The psychology of the unthinkable: Taboo trade-offs, forbidden base rates, and heretical counterfactuals. *Journal of Personality and Social Psychology, 78*(5), 853–70.

Chapter 4: Stories and Situations

1. Chater, N., & Loewenstein, G. (2016). The under-appreciated drive for sense-making. *Journal of Economic Behavior & Organization, 126*(2), 137–54.

2. Butcher, F., Gore, A., Shortland, N., & Maxwell, I. (2011). Scoping study to further understand the collection of 'Pattern of Life' information for C-IED operators. DSTL/CR60093. Final customer report, Porton, Wiltshire: Dstl Porton Down.

3. Mercier, H., & Sperber, D. (2011). Why do humans reason? Arguments for an argumentative theory. *Behavioral and Brain Sciences*, 34(2), 57–74.
4. American Rhetoric (n.d.). George W. Bush: The deliberate and deadly attacks ...were acts of war. President's address from cabinet room following cabinet meeting, 12 September 2001. Retrieved from http://www.americanrhetoric.com/speeches/gwbush911cabinetroomaddress.htm (accessed 23 May 2021).
5. Twomey, S. (Dec. 2016). How (almost) everyone failed to prepare for Pearl Harbor. Retrieved from https://www.smithsonianmag.com/history/how-almost-everyone-failed-prepare-pearl-harbor-1-180961144/ (accessed 23 May 2021); Martin, V. B. (2015). The system was blinking red: Awareness contexts and disasters. *Grounded Theory Review*, 14(2), 11–21; De Bruijn, H. (2006). One fight, one team: The 9/11 commission report on intelligence, fragmentation and information. *Public Administration*, 84(2), 267–87.
6. Kean, T. H., & Hamilton, L. H. (2004). *The 9/11 Report*. St. Martin's Press.
7. Ibid, 336 and 344.
8. Gottschall, J. (2012). *The Storytelling Animal: How Stories Make Us Human*. Houghton Mifflin Harcourt.

Chapter 5: Time Mastery

1. Bowden, M. (2012). *The Finish: The Killing of Osama Bin Laden*. Atlantic Monthly Press.
2. Gans Jr., J. A. (10 Oct. 2012). 'This is 50-50': Behind Obama's decision to kill Bin Laden. *The Atlantic*. Retrieved from https://www.theatlantic.com/international/archive/2012/10/this-is-50-50-behind-obamas-decision-to-kill-bin-laden/263449/ (accessed 23 May 2021).

3. Madden, G. J., Begotka, A. M., Raiff, B. R., & Kastern, L. L. (2003). Delay discounting of real and hypothetical rewards. *Experimental and Clinical Psychopharmacology, 11*(2), 139–45.

4. Tetlock, P. E. (2003). Thinking the unthinkable: Sacred values and taboo cognitions. *Trends in Cognitive Science, 7*(7), 320–4.

5. Shortland, N. D., McGarry, P., Thompson, L., Stevens, C., & Alison, L. J. (2021). The effect of a 3-minute mindfulness intervention, and the mediating role of maximization, on critical incident decision-making. *Frontiers in Psychology, 12.*

6. Alison, L., Doran, B., Long, M. L., Power, N., & Humphrey, A. (2013). The effects of subjective time pressure and individual differences on hypotheses generation and action prioritization in police investigations. *Journal of Experimental Psychology: Applied, 19*(1), 83–93.

7. Shortland, N., Thompson, L., & Alison, L. (2020). Police perfection: Examining the effect of trait maximization on police decision-making. *Frontiers in Psychology, 11.*

Chapter 6: Adaptation

1. Kruglanski, A. W., Webster, D. M., & Klem, A. (1993). Motivated resistance and openness to persuasion in the presence or absence of prior information. *Journal of Personality and Social Psychology, 65*(5), 861–76.

2. Houghton, D. (2013). *The Decision Point: Six Cases in U.S. Foreign Policy Decision Making.* Oxford University Press.

3. Alison, L., Doran, B., Long, M. L., Power, N., & Humphrey, A. (2013). The effects of subjective time pressure and individual differences on hypotheses generation and action prioritization in police investigations. *Journal of Experimental Psychology: Applied, 19*(1), 83–93.

4. Ibid.
5. Simon, H. A. (1956). Rational choice and the structure of the environment. *Psychological Review*, *63*(1), 129–38.
6. Tversky, A., & Kahneman, D. (1973). Availability: A heuristic for judging frequency and probability. *Cognitive Psychology*, *5*(2), 207–32; Tversky, A., & Kahneman, D. (1974). Judgment under uncertainty: Heuristics and biases. *Science*, *185*(4157), 1124–31.

Chapter 7: Redirecting the Trolley

1. Tom, S. M., Fox, C. R., Trepel, C., & Poldrack, R. A. (2007). The neural basis of loss aversion in decision-making under risk. *Science*, *315*(5811), 515–8.
2. Deakin, J. M., & Cobley, S. (2003). An examination of the practice environments in figure skating and volleyball: A search for deliberate practice. *Expert Performance in Sports*, 90–113.
3. Duckworth, A. L., Peterson, C., Matthews, M. D., & Kelly, D. R. (2007). Grit: Perseverance and passion for long term goals. *Journal of Personality and Social Psychology*, *92*(6), 1087–101.
4. Ibid.
5. Kelly, D. R., Matthews, M. D., & Bartone, P. T. (2014). Grit and hardiness as predictors of performance among West Point cadets. *Military Psychology*, *26*(4), 327–42.
6. Olivola, C. Y. (2018). The interpersonal sunk-cost effect. *Psychological Science*, *29*, 1072–83.
7. Howard, M. C., & Crayne, M. P. (2019). Persistence: Defining the multidimensional construct and creating a measure. *Personality and Individual Differences*, *139*, 77–89.
8. Gillett, R. (18 May 2015). From welfare to one of the world's wealthiest women – the incredible rags-to-riches story of J.K. Rowling. *Business Insider*. Retrieved from

https://www.businessinsider.com/the-rags-to-riches-story-of-jk-rowling-2015-5 (accessed 23 May 2021).

9. Moss, S. (28 Sep. 2009). Ricky Gervais: 'Before The Office I never tried hard at anything'. *The Guardian*. Retrieved from https://www.theguardian.com/lifeandstyle/2009/sep/28/ricky-gervais-the-office (accessed 23 May 2021).

Chapter 8: Resilience and Recovery

1. Elliott, S. (2003). 'The Media Business: Advertising; 'Takes a licking and keeps on ticking' is on the way out at Timex. Now, it's 'Life is ticking.' *The New York Times*. Retrieved from: https://www.nytimes.com/2003/08/26/business/media-business-advertising-takes-licking-keeps-ticking-way-timex-now-it-s-life.html (accessed 23 May 2021)

2. British Medical Association (2020). COVID-19 – ethical issues. A guidance note. Retrieved from https://www.bma.org.uk/media/2226/bma-covid-19-ethics-guidance.pdf (accessed 23 May 2021).

3. Elliott, E., Ezra-Nevo, G., Regev, L., Neufeld-Cohen, A., & Chen, A. (2010). Resilience to social stress coincides with functional DNA methylation of the Crf gene in adult mice. *Nature Neuroscience*, *13*(11), 1351–3.

4. Hone, L. (Aug. 2019). 3 secrets of resilient people. TED Talk [video]. Retrieved from https://www.ted.com/talks/lucy_hone_3_secrets_of_resilient_people?language=en (accessed 23 May 2021).

5. Napier, C. (18 Dec. 2020). What is the Serenity Prayer? Is it biblical? Christianity.com. Retrieved from https://www.christianity.com/wiki/prayer/what-is-the-serenity-prayer-is-it-biblical.html (accessed 23 May 2021).

6. Hone, L. (Aug. 2019). 3 secrets of resilient people. TED Talk [video]. Retrieved from https://www.ted.com/talks/lucy_hone_3_secrets_of_resilient_people?language=en (accessed 23 May 2021).

Acknowledgements

Laurence:

It's a little bizarre writing a book about critical incidents during an 18-month period of a global, once-in-a-hundred-years, critical incident. You see, all around you, and on a daily basis, decision makers (politicians, medical professionals, academics, friends, family and neighbours) grapple with decisions. For me, it's highlighted two things: (i) the absolute importance of understanding critical incident decision-making, and (ii) an acute awareness of who you can and can't rely on. Some people step up, some don't move and some people step back. I'd like to thank those in the first category for doing the right thing at the right time. Critical incidents bring into sharp relief people's deep and underlying value systems and how they will behave. They quickly reveal the core of a person.

All of the following are so clearly in the step forward category:

Neil is a fun person to work with – generous with his time, compassion and energy. Perhaps, like me, he is a bit of an outsider in terms of the general academic community. However, there is something to be said for very clear goal orientation, especially when it is directed at solving real problems rather than chasing citations or belonging to the most recent 'exclusive' academic club. Thank you for inspiring me, supporting me and staying true.

I'm also grateful to Michael Humann, who is the fulcrum around which The Ground Truth team operates. He is unflappable, rock solid and a true friend. Thank you for your patience, endurance and wisdom.

Thanks to Frankie, Fergie, Ricardo, Paul, Hayley, Simon and, of course, to Emily, my wife. Ems is not only in the step forward category but is a bigger person than me and can more easily forgive those in the 'not move' and 'step back' categories.

Also to Mark Fallon, Al McGregor, Sarah Chapman Trim, David Burke, Spence, Steve Kleinman, Sarah Robertson, John Short, David Hitchcock, Andrew Richmond, Cath Hamilton, Karl Walsh, Joe Poitier and Iain Buchan. You've held me together on various projects and recharged my battery at critical times where others have drained it. It's good to know there is plenty of good out there among the bad.

Neil:

This book represents a ten-year journey of seeking to understand how people make decisions in the real world, and along this path a lot of people have taken a chance on me, supported me or generally assisted in bringing this work to the world. First and foremost, I owe it all to Laurence. From meeting all those years ago as a prospective student interviewing for his MSc programme to our work now as collaborators, there is not another academic on this planet I would rather work alongside. You truly show what making a difference means, without ever sacrificing the scientific depth or rigor of what you do. It is awe-inspiring to see the impact you have had on the world. While many people sat back, you lead the charge to support those in need and worked tirelessly to help the global response to Covid-19 however you could. I am glad the world finally noticed and (finally!) gave you that MBE you deserve. Most importantly, I am grateful to have you as a friend. Much of the advice we give in this book is advice you have given me over the years and I, for one, can attest to how useful it is. I'm proud of our work together, but I'm even more excited for what comes next.

This work is also closely tied to some of our research in the United States with the Army Research Institute (ARI) for the Behavioral and Social Sciences Foundational Science Research Unit. A lot of the studies and research we used as a foundation for this book come from their support and I am indebted to Gregory Ruark, Maureen McCusker, Garett Howardson, Alexander Wind and Nikki Blacksmith. I am not sure what expectations Greg had when I called him out of the blue in 2016 with an idea about military indecision, but I am forever grateful that he gave us a chance to study it. Beyond the team at ARI, we are incredibly fortunate to have a number of people in our corner who have been immensely kind in supporting and facilitating our work: Sarah Chapman Trim, Martin Ferguson, David Burke, Frankie Surmon-Bohr, Michael Humann, Lisa Thompson, just to name a few.

Over the past 18 months, like many of us, I have had to attend far too many events via Zoom. Writing this book has been a helpful distraction from the immense sorrow of not seeing those I love. To all my best friends, and the next generation (Aari, Olivia, Frank, Ernie and Alfred), I can't wait to see you and celebrate our many milestones together. To my family, I miss you every day.

Finally, to my wife and the entire Wu family. Thank you for the love, food, support and keeping me humble by reminding me that I am not a 'real' doctor.

Collectively, we would like to thank Joanna Moorhead for keeping us on the straight and narrow and helping us bring our work to life; Marta Catalano, Emma Owen and Penguin Random House for offering us this opportunity and shaping our thoughts; and Julia Kellaway for making sure that we communicate what matters the most, to those who need it.

Index